# Kim J. A

# What
# God
# Hates

## Proverbs 6:16-19

**ISBN:** 9781796688979

*Dedicated to all who Hate what the LORD Hates*

*Abhor what is evil. (Romans 12:9)*

# CONTENTS

# CHAPTER 1
# OVERVIEW OF WHAT GOD HATES

A re you aware that God hates certain things? There are six specific things listed by Solomon that God hates. Wait, no, there are seven. Yes, there are seven things that are an abomination to Him. We find them listed here in Proverbs 6:16-19. Read these verses very carefully and perhaps even with a little personal conviction - ouch!

**Proverbs 6:16-19**

*16 These six things the Lord hates, Yes, seven are an abomination to Him: 17 A proud look, A lying tongue, Hands that shed innocent blood, 18 A heart that devises wicked plans, Feet that are swift in running to evil, 19 A false witness who speaks lies, And one who sows discord among brethren.*

The Catholic Church divides sins into venial, or less serious, sins and mortal sins, which threaten the soul with eternal damnation unless absolved before death through confession and penitence.

It holds mortal sins to be "grave violations of the Ten Commandments and the Beatitudes", including murder, contraception, abortion, perjury, adultery, and lust.

The Catechism of the Catholic Church states that "immediately after death the souls of those who die in a state of mortal sin descend into Hell".

Although there is no definitive list of mortal sins, many accept the broad, seven deadly sins or capital vices laid down in the 6th century by Pope Gregory the Great (590 AD) and popularized in the Middle Ages by Dante in *The Inferno*.

Perhaps you grew up hearing about The Seven Deadly Sins! Are you able to name the original Seven Deadly Sins? Are you aware of what the original punishment was for the Seven Deadly Sins? Allow me to share with you the list and the punishment that followed.

### The Original Seven Deadly Sins and Their Punishments

1. **Pride** - Broken on the wheel.
2. **Envy** - Put in freezing water.
3. **Gluttony** - Forced to eat rats, toads, and snakes.
4. **Lust** - Smothered in fire and brimstone.
5. **Anger** - Dismembered alive.
6. **Greed** - Put in cauldrons of boiling oil.
7. **Sloth** - Thrown in snake pits.

In researching these sins I discovered that in 2008 the Catholic Church updated *The Seven Deadly Sins*. They stated that because of the age of globalization, there were now seven new sins that needed to be added to the original list. It was stated that "the Pope deplored the 'decreasing sense of sin' in today's 'secularized world' and the falling numbers of Roman Catholics going to confession." Today it is estimated that 60% of Catholics no longer go to confession in Italy. One of the bishops of the Catholic Church said that new sins are because of globalization (we have a much smaller world) and that these sins are not individual in nature, but they now affect all of society. So what are the New Seven Deadly Sins of the Catholic Church? They are:

1. Environmental pollution.
2. Genetic manipulation.
3. Accumulating excessive wealth.
4. Inflicting poverty.
5. Drug trafficking and consumption.
6. Morally debatable experiments.
7. Violation of fundamental rights of human nature.

What a list. So, we now have fourteen sins that will send you to hell if left unconfessed and without proper penitence. Now, having shared this, I can tell you based on the authority of God's Word that all sin, whatever sin it is, has the ability to send you to hell. However, the gravest of all sins is the sin of rejection of Jesus Christ. To reject the person of Jesus Christ as one's SAVIOR is to secure one's spot in hell. The entire message of the Bible is a message of God redeeming mankind. Do not reject Jesus Christ – He is the WAY, the TRUTH, and the LIFE, and no one will stand before God without going through Him (John 14:6).

The purpose of this book is NOT to speak about lesser sins, or greater sins, but to actually teach about *the seven things that the LORD hates* which are found in the book of Proverbs. All seven of the things the LORD hates are, in fact, sin. Sin categorized by Pope Gregory can be found in the Bible, but I want us to take a look at the *seven things the LORD hates,* as found here in Proverbs 6.

In this first chapter I want us to take a quick overview of all seven things the LORD hates, and then in the chapters that follow we will look at them individually. Now, are you ready to dig into God's Word and learn about the things the LORD hates? Here we go!

The first thing you will need to do is to put this book down and go and get your Bible. Next, you will need to turn to Proverbs 6 and read verses 16-19. These three verses provide for us the list of the seven things the LORD hates; another way of saying this is, the seven sins that are an abomination to God.

You also might want to grab a pen. I want you to underline the word *"abomination"* in verse 16. What is the definition of this word? It is important that we fully understand the words we are looking at in this text.

Abomination: "Something disgusting (morally), i.e. (as a noun) an abhorrence; especially idolatry or (concretely) an idol:-- abominable (custom, thing), abomination." (Hebrew word: *tow`ebah*,    to-ay-baw')[1]

### Understanding the Word Abomination

1. There are things that the Lord literally feels extreme enmity toward.
2. There are things that the Lord literally has a strong aversion to and finds very distasteful.
3. There are things that the Lord literally expresses or feels extreme enmity or active hostility toward.
4. There are things that the Lord literally has a deep, shuddering repugnance for.
5. There are things that the Lord literally finds disgusting.
6. There are things that the Lord literally has utter disgust & intolerance for.
7. There are things that the Lord literally and strongly detests.
8. There are things that the Lord literally and morally condemns.[2]

Were you aware that God can hate? Yes, there are some very specific items that God hates. (Other places in the Scripture where we are told that God hates: Deuteronomy 16:22; Psalm 45:7; Revelation 2:6).

When Solomon writes, *"These six things the LORD hates, Yes, seven are an abomination to Him"*, this is what is known as sequential numbering. This method of writing was used to get one's attention. You see this done several times in Proverbs.

Now, underline the word "seven" used here in verse 16. The number seven is not being used for perfection, as some think, but as completion. God completely hates these seven things found in verses 16-19. We would be wise to place them on our hate list as well. The writer of Ecclesiastes tells us that there is a *"time to hate"* (Ecclesiastes 3:8).

So then, what are the Seven Sins that God Hates?

**I. A Proud Look – v. 17**

Take a moment and write in the margin of your Bible the word "Pride".

*"A proud look, A lying tongue, Hands that shed innocent blood,"*

What is a proud look? Allow me to tell you what this is not, first. This word is not speaking about our accomplishments, but about our demeanor/behavior. It is speaking about the way in which we carry ourselves in a public setting. Another way of saying this is, "haughty eyes, or lofty eyes."

The truth of the matter is…

- We ought to be proud of our children's achievements.
- We ought to be proud of our military.
- We ought to be proud of any special recognition we may have received.

Please understand that this is not what this verse is speaking about. It is okay to be proud of certain achievements in life.

So, what does it mean here? It is speaking about the other type of being proud. This type of pride is pride that you are better than others. Take a moment and circle the middle letter in pride – it is "I". This is what God hates!

Now, on the other hand, if your children's achievements lead you to think your children are better than others, then you have crossed the line from a healthy form of being proud to something which God hates. If our military is placed on a pedestal, then we have moved into the other realm of being proud, and God hates it! If our own achievements in life cause us to believe that we are better than others, then we have stepped over into an evil type of being proud, and God hates it.

If you believe that you are better than others around you, you are carrying about within you a pride that God hates. Dr. McGee wrote, "It is the attitude that overvalues self and undervalues others."

The Apostle Paul wrote to the Romans,

*"For I say, through the grace given to me, to everyone who is among you, not to think of himself more highly than he ought to think, but to think soberly, as God has dealt to each one a measure of faith."* (Romans 12:3)

The issue of the proud look in this verse goes much deeper than a casual reading. The proud look believes that you can do life without God, or that you are your own god. There are many people today who want nothing to do with God – they say that they don't need Him. Others believe that once man split the atom and returned from the moon we proved that we are god!

Simply put, a proud individual doesn't see his need for God's grace. Are you aware that this sin will send people to hell? And if you think that you are so good that you don't need Jesus Christ, your sin of pride will send you to hell.

By the way, in chapters to come we will not only look at that which God hates, but we will see how we are to counter each of these things that God hates. It's not enough to see what God hates; we need to see how we can be more than overcomers.

What is the second sin God hates?

## II. A Lying Tongue – v. 17

In your own Bible write the word, "Lying".

*"A proud look, A lying tongue, Hands that shed innocent blood,"*

I don't know about you, but I don't like being lied to. Several years ago I caught several Christian people who had lied to my face. Can I tell you that God hates lying? We read here that it is an abomination to Him!

In a recent poll, 91% of those who responded said that they lie routinely, and 75% of them said that they lie to their best friends regularly.[3]

In Exodus 20, that passage where we find the Ten Commandments, we read,

*"You shall not bear false witness against your neighbor."* (Exodus 20:16)

It seems to me that we live in a world where people love to lie about their neighbors. It has almost become a sport! I challenge you NOT to accept everything someone tells you about another person – it just may be a lie!

God tells us in His Word that He hates lying! No if's, and's, or but's about it. You and I ought to HATE it, too.

Paul wrote in Romans 12:9b,

*Abhor what is evil.*

The word *abhor* means to hate. We are to hate what is evil. Understand that evil is based on what God says and NOT on what people legalize! I hope we will accept this as truth!

The Psalmist prayed,

*"Deliver my soul, O LORD, from lying lips And from a deceitful tongue."* (Psalm 120:2)

## Who Are You Most Like?

According to John 8, the devil is a liar and the father of all lies (John 8:44). I tell people all the time that we are no more like God than when we speak TRUTH, and no more like the devil than when we speak LIES. He is a LIAR and the father of LIES!

*"You are of your father the devil, and the desires of your father you want to do. He was a murderer from the beginning, and does not stand in the truth, because there is no truth in him. When he speaks a lie, he speaks from his own resources, for he is a liar and the father of it."* (John 8:44)

When we became Christians there were certain things that we were to put off – as if they were soiled clothes (dirty clothes). Paul writes,

*"Lie not one to another, seeing that ye have put off the old man with his deeds;"* (Colossians 3:9)

Paul also penned the following words (under the inspiration of the Holy Spirit),

*"Therefore, putting away lying, "Let each one of you speak truth with his neighbor," for we are members of one another."* (Ephesians 4:25)

H.A. Ironside wrote, "False words bespeak a deceitful heart.'

What is the third sin God hates?

### III. Hands That Shed Innocent Blood – v. 17

Now, write in the margin of your Bible the word, "Murder".

*"A proud look, A lying tongue, <u>Hands that shed innocent blood</u>,"*

Doesn't it make you sick when you hear about someone like Joseph Duncan who has killed innocent people? It really bothers me that this man has not been executed. We would have a lot fewer murders in the U.S. if we would quickly execute those who commit such heinous crimes against humanity.

Do you hate the fact that here in the United States of America 24,359 people were murdered in 2020 according to the CDC?

### Cities of Refugee

In researching this idea about shedding innocent blood I discovered that this had to do with the establishment of the cities of refuge mentioned in the Old Testament. Suppose you were out chopping wood, and as you were swinging the axe, the axe head flew off and hit your neighbor and killed him. His family might want to take immediate revenge because of his death. God had Israel set up cities of refuge for people to flee to so that they could explain what happened to judges, and the judges would determine the punishment if any.

Here, in the case of the cities of refuge shedding innocent blood is when someone kills another person at the scene of an accident, and they are unaware of all the details surrounding the death.

### Saul's Hatred of David

How many of us have read about King Saul's hatred of David? Here we have a picture of one man who was bent on killing, an innocent man. Pause and go read: I Samuel 19. Saul was constantly looking for someone who would betray David. If someone would have stepped forward, it would have been equivalent to shedding innocent blood.

### Murder of Ishbosheth

Here is another example of men shedding innocent blood in the Old Testament. Some of David's men sought to protect David by killing the members of Saul's household. They saw them as a threat to David. In II Sam. 4 we read that some men came into the house of Ishbosheth and killed him while he was sleeping on his bed.

They cut off his head and brought it to David. David was not pleased and told them that they had killed an innocent man. David had these men executed for their crime of stabbing to death an innocent man.

The point is, God hates those who murder, and who take the lives of innocent people. You and I ought to hate what God hates. I am so sick of how people will value the life of the murderer once he/she is on trial – what a twisted and perverse society. Doesn't anyone think BIBLICALLY anymore?

What is the fourth sin God hates?

### IV. A Heart that Devises Wicked Plans – v. 18

Now write in the margin of your Bible the word, "Wickedness".

*"A heart that devises wicked plans, Feet that are swift in running to evil,"*

Here we are looking at thoughts of iniquity. How ugly is the human heart at times? We can allow our hearts to THINK about some terrible things. We can commit some violent acts in our minds. It has been said, "What is played in the theatre of the mind will eventually be played out in the theatre of life." Therefore, as followers of Jesus Christ, we must hate what God hates.

Jesus taught about the heart in the book of Matthew. He said that everything about us as man flows from the heart – the essence of who and what we are as people.

As believers, we must nix the evil sin of our thought life. Everything in our mind must be brought into captivity unto the obedience of Christ (II Corinthians 10:5). It is wrong for us to dwell in the realm of evil imaginations, or evil mischief. It is WRONG for us to plan to do evil toward others.

I want us to pause for just a moment and think about how many crimes began in the human heart! What crime doesn't begin in the heart of man?

Consider what Jesus taught,

*"But those things which proceed out of the mouth come from the heart, and they defile a man. For out of the heart proceed evil thoughts, murders, adulteries, fornications, thefts, false witness, blasphemies."* (Matthew 15:18-19)

God tells us that He hates – no, it is an abomination – for those who allow their hearts to devise wicked plans.

What everyone needs today is a heart transplant. They need a new heart! Listen to this fantastic verse from the book of Ezekiel. We read,

*"A new heart also will I give you, and a new spirit will I put within you: and I will take away the stony heart out of your flesh, and I will give you an heart of flesh."* (Ezekiel 36:26)

Hear me – God is in the business of helping us to THINK about good things, and not evil. We are challenged throughout the Scripture to dwell on that which is good. I challenge all of us, including myself; to pull down that which exalts itself against God. Don't allow your mind to go there any longer.

What is the fifth sin God hates?

## V. Feet that are Swift in Running to Evil – v. 18

Once again write in the margin of your Bible the word, "Evil".

*"A heart that devises wicked plans, <u>Feet that are swift in running to evil,</u>"*

It has been said that "feet follow where the heart has already been." How true it is! Perhaps you have found it true in your life as well. Do you know anyone who seems to always allow their feet to take them into evil? I know that I can name a few people whom my path has crossed. One such person I know recently landed himself in jail. Several others that I know are only one additional step away from judgment day!

In Proverbs 1:16, we read,

*For their feet run to evil, And they make haste to shed blood.*

The prophet Isaiah penned the following words,

*Their feet run to evil, And they make haste to shed innocent blood; Their thoughts are thoughts of iniquity; Wasting and destruction are in their paths.* (Isaiah 59:7)

Are you aware that the Bible teaches that *"bad company corrupts good morals"*? (I Corinthians 15:33). If you are friends with someone who only runs into evil, then it is time for you to make different friends. It has been said, "Friends determine the direction and the quality of your life."[4] If you are involved in evil things (things contrary to the holiness of God) then it is time you STOP in your tracks and make some necessary changes. Take the high road! Always take the road of Holiness!

Peer pressure is powerful – as a follower of Jesus Christ, you and I are to be the more powerful peer! Friends influence one another, but the believer is to be the more powerful influencer! Instead of having feet that are swift in running to evil, we ought to have feet that are swift to run into the presence of God Almighty!

What is the sixth sin God hates?

**VI. A False Witness That Speaks Lies – v. 19**

Now, write in the margin of your Bible the word, "Falsehoods".

*"A false witness who speaks lies, And one who sows discord among brethren."*

Please note that what we have first is a *"false witness"*. When someone lies under oath in a court of law it is called perjury. We witnessed this with former President Bill Clinton, and we saw it recently in the Casey Anthony trial. I don't know about you, but I am tired of the slanderous lies people tell.

Did you notice that twice in these three verses we are told that God HATES (it is an abomination) lying? In verse 17, we have someone who lies through their teeth, and in verse 19, we have someone lying through their teeth against another individual. Are you aware that Jesus faced this type of lying?

One guy that I was reading stated that this type of lying now has a new name. It is called: *Strategic Misrepresentation or Reality Augmentation."* Can you believe it?

Have you ever been falsely accused? How did it make you feel? Don't you HATE IT when someone lies about you? Of course, you do!

I already mentioned that Jesus had false witnesses who spoke lies about him, but are you aware that so did Stephen, the first martyr (Acts 6:8-15), and so did the Apostle Paul (Acts 24:9, 25:7)?

In Psalm 101:5 we read,

*"Whoever secretly slanders his neighbor, Him I will destroy; The one who has a haughty look and a proud heart, Him I will not endure."*

God hates those who are false witnesses, who speak lies, and so should we. I challenge you NOT TO PUT UP WITH IT! Not at home, not at school, and not in the church.

What is the seventh sin God hates?

**VII. One Who Sows Discord Among Brethren – v. 19**

Finally, I want you to write in the margin of your Bible the word, "Discord".

*"A false witness who speaks lies, <u>And one who sows discord among brethren."</u>*

Discord hurts everyone! Say that out loud to yourself: Discord hurts everyone!

Are you aware that not everyone who sets foot in the church necessarily has the best interest of the church body in mind? There are some people who are just bent on causing problems within the church. You have to wonder if these people are truly saved!

I have discovered as a pastor that most issues that arise in the church are over personalities, or over personal desires. When someone is not getting their way they go on the defense and begin to sow discord within the body of Christ. If you ever find yourself trying to get people within the church to stand with you on a certain decision, and you make remarks that are defamatory against another brother/sister in Christ, then you are sowing discord among brethren.

Stirring the brethren up is something that God hates! We ought to hate it too! I've seen it here in this church, and it broke my heart then, and I continue to weep today.

Allow me to tell you that it is never right to destroy a church - never! If your behavior leads to church division, a church split, then you are guilty of sowing discord. It would be better for you to walk away quietly than to destroy God's church. And please don't tell me that you are the sacred guardian of God's church. That is the job of the Holy Spirit - not you!

Jesus told us that the opposite of sowing discord is peacemaking! As a matter of fact, in the beatitudes, we read,

*"Blessed are the peacemakers, For they shall be called sons of God."* (Matthew 5:9)

## Wrap Up

So, what is the answer to these sins?

1. The Lord hates eyes that are full of pride: Humble yourself.
2. The Lord hates a tongue that spews lies: Tell the truth.

3. The Lord hates the hand that takes innocent life: Value life.
4. The Lord hates a heart that devises wicked schemes: Oppose evil.
5. The Lord hates feet that rush into evil: Watch your step.
6. The Lord hates a false witness: Testify about others truthfully.
7. The Lord hates a man who causes arguments: Promote peace.

Do you need to repent (change your mind) of any of these sins we have considered today? Why not do it now? Walk away from this first chapter in humility – dependence upon God. Walk away from this first chapter as a Christian who will speak the truth – set lies behind you. Walk away from this first chapter respecting all life. Walk away from this first chapter allowing the Holy Spirit to control your thoughts. Walk away from this first chapter committed to avoiding pathways of evil. Walk away from this first chapter determined that you will not be a false witness and pass on lies about others. Walk away from this first chapter resolved that you will not sow discord in any church body. Finally, walk away from reading this first chapter hating those things that God hates!

End Notes:

[1] Hebrew meaning of the word, "abomination".

[2] Daniel P. Johnson

[3] A poll that I came across on the internet.

[4] Andy Stanley

# CHAPTER 2
# A PROUD LOOK

W ithout looking back at the previous chapter can you name the original Seven Deadly Sins presented by Pope Gregory the Great in the 6<sup>th</sup> century? What about the revised or updated list of Seven Modern Sins? Okay, go ahead and look back at chapter one.

Our focus for this book will not be the original Seven Deadly Sins, but the Seven Things the LORD Hates, or the seven sins that God hates as found in Proverbs 6:16-19.

In the previous chapter, we did a quick tour of the Seven Things the LORD Hates. In this chapter, and the chapters that follow, we will look at the Seven Things the LORD Hates individually and dig deeper into each one of them.

In this chapter, we are going to take a look at the first of the Seven Things the LORD Hates.

First, God Hates a Proud Look – v. 17

If you have already done this step you can skip it; if not, I want you to write in the margin of your own Bible the word, "Pride".

The KJV and the NKJV read,

*"A proud look,"*

The New American Standard reads,

*"Haughty eyes,"*

The Bible in Basic English,

*"Eyes of pride,"*

**I. What Pride Is Not.**

I believe that it is important for us to understand what this sin is not. Pride is not…

- Self-esteem – feeling good about yourself. Satisfaction in a job well done – doing all for God's glory.
- Rejoicing in honor given.

It is only if we allow our self-esteem to rise to the level of our thinking that we are better than others around us, or if we would allow ourselves to believe that we are the only ones capable of doing a good job in certain areas, or if in giving honor we do so to win the favor of certain people.

There is nothing wrong with positive self-esteem, being proud of a job well done, or giving honor to whom honor is due.

**II. What Pride Is**

What is meant by "A proud look"? Perhaps a better translation would be *haughty eyes*, or *lofty eyes*. Earlier I asked you to write the word "Pride" in the margin of your Bible. What is pride? It is the attitude that says that "I am better than you are." Remember the middle letter in PRIDE is 'I'.

Dr. McGee wrote, "It is the attitude that overvalues self and under-values others."

C.S. Lewis wrote that, "Pride is mankind's greatest sin."

Someone said the following about pride: "Pride is the only disease that makes everyone sick but the one who has it." Why is that? Because the person with pride is usually oblivious that they are prideful – not in all cases, but in most. Pride blinds a person!

The word, *"haughty"* in Hebrew literally means, "to be lifted up." This describes the person who has exalted himself/herself above others and is looking down on them. We have created expressions in our language for pointing out the person full of pride. Here are some examples:

- That individual is riding their high horse.
- They are looking down their nose at us.
- Surely that person is stuck up.

However, I believe the issue of the "proud look" here in this verse goes much deeper. It is the "proud look" of believing that you can do life without God, or that you are your own god. Simply put, a PROUD individual doesn't see his need for God's grace. Are you aware that this sin will send people to hell?

Have you ever thought of where this awful sin originated?

### III. Who Originated the Sin of Pride – Isaiah 14:12-15

It has been said, "Pride was the first sin in heaven." I want us to see how true that statement is. Open your personal Bible to Isaiah, the fourteenth chapter. The sin of pride originated with a cherub angel by the name of Lucifer.

#### Isaiah 14:12-15

*"12 "How you are fallen from heaven, O Lucifer, son of the morning! How you are cut down to the ground, You who weakened the nations! 13 For you have said in your heart: 'I will ascend into heaven, I will exalt my*

*throne above the stars of God; I will also sit on the mount of the congrega-*
*tion On the farthest sides of the north; 14 I will ascend above the heights of*
*the clouds, I will be like the Most High.' 15 Yet you shall be brought down*
*to Sheol, To the lowest depths of the Pit."*

This passage of Scripture is describing for us where sin was first
introduced, and more specifically with whom PRIDE originated. In
the book of Ezekiel, in the twenty-eight chapter, we discover that
Lucifer was actually a cherub angel. Many theologians believe that
he was the angel who was in charge of all worship in heaven and
that his body may have been a musical instrument. We do know
that it was a cherub that was placed at the entrance of the garden
after The Fall (Genesis 3) and that they played a significant role in
the Tabernacle, and specifically the Holy of Holies. In the book of
Revelation, they appear to be the four living creatures (Revelation
4).

### The Five "I Will's" of Lucifer

Before us in Isaiah 14, we read some five times that Lucifer desired
to place Himself above God. That's PRIDE! Look with me at the
five times in these verses:

1. *I will ascend into heaven.*
2. *I will exalt my throne above the stars of God.*
3. *I will also sit on the mount of the congregation.*
4. *I will ascend above the heights of the clouds.*
5. *I will be like the Most High.*

What Lucifer was saying here in this passage is that he didn't need
God and that he was better than God. As a matter of fact, in Ezekiel
28:2, he said, "I am god." Lucifer was seeking to usurp the
authority of God Almighty. He wanted to take the place of God.
This is what pride seeks to do!

### IV. How the Sin of Pride Is Seen in the Bible

The sin of PRIDE is found throughout the Bible. I want to provide you with a list of some nine different individuals who allowed PRIDE to destroy their lives. I won't be writing lengthy comments. However, I would suggest that you do some additional research on these individuals if one of them strikes a chord with you.

1. Pharaoh – *"And Pharaoh said, "Who is the LORD, that I should obey His voice to let Israel go? I do not know the LORD, nor will I let Israel go."* (Exodus 5:2)

2. Naaman – *"But Naaman became furious, and went away and said, "Indeed, I said to myself, 'He will surely come out to me, and stand and call on the name of the LORD his God, and wave his hand over the place, and heal the leprosy."* (II Kings 5:11)

3. Uzziah – *"But when he was strong his heart was lifted up, to his destruction, for he transgressed against the LORD his God by entering the temple of the LORD to burn incense on the altar of incense."* (II Chronicles 26:16)

4. Hezekiah – *"But Hezekiah did not repay according to the favor shown him, for his heart was lifted up; therefore wrath was looming over him and over Judah and Jerusalem."* (II Chronicles 32:25)

5. Haman – *"When Haman saw that Mordecai did not bow or pay him homage, Haman was filled with wrath."* (Esther 3:5)

6. Nebuchadnezzar – *"The king spoke, saying, "Is not this great Babylon, that I have built for a royal dwelling by my mighty power and for the honor of my majesty?"* (Daniel 4:30)

7. Belshazzar – *"And you have lifted yourself up against the Lord of heaven. They have brought the vessels of His house before you, and you and your lords, your wives and your concubines, have drunk wine from them."* (Daniel 5:23a)

8. Judah – *"The pride of your heart has deceived you, You who dwell in the clefts of the rock, Whose habitation is high; You who say in your heart, 'Who will bring me down to the ground?"* (Obadiah 1:3)

9. Pharisee – *"The Pharisee stood and prayed thus with himself, 'God, I thank You that I am not like other men--extortioners, unjust, adulterers, or even as this tax collector. I fast twice a week; I give tithes of all that I possess."* (Luke 18:11-12)

## V. The Ways to Overcome the Sin of Pride

Now let's take a look at five ways for us to overcome this sin of pride. They are:

1. Pay close attention to your attitude.

If you begin to believe that you are better than others, then you are boasting a prideful spirit. You have an attitude of haughtiness about you, and you need to do something about it.

The author of Proverbs also wrote,

*"The fear of the LORD is to hate evil; Pride and arrogance and the evil way And the perverse mouth I hate."* (Prov. 8:13)

In Proverbs 21:4 we read,

*"A haughty look, a proud heart, And the plowing of the wicked are sin."*

In the New Testament, we read,

*"God resisteth the proud, but giveth grace unto the humble."* (James 4:6)

Attitude is EVERYTHING – therefore, watch your attitude.

2. Don't believe all your press reports.

Often it is when people make a fuss over us that we begin to get puffed up (i.e., stars, sports figures, music people, and even Christian celebrities). When wonderful things are being said about us, or to us, we need to quickly move on. Say, "Thanks", but move on quickly! Reveling in your press has the ability to produce in us a PRIDEFUL heart.

The Bible says,

*"For in him we live, and move, and have our being;"* (Acts 17:28)

We are who we are because of WHOSE we are! Don't you FORGET it!

In Proverbs 16:15, we read,

*"Pride goes before destruction, And a haughty spirit before a fall."*

Many people have allowed PRIDE to well up in them, and it has only led to their demise. Did you hear the words PRIDE and HAUGHTY in that verse? And did you also grasp the words, DESTRUCTION, and FALL?

It's nice to have people make a big "do" over us at times, but we need to be careful that we don't paste all the headlines on some bulletin board. Many believers have fallen flat on their faces because they began to think that they were too big for their britches! Yes, it is possible to TRIP over the words people are saying about us.

3. Your behavior may signal PRIDE in your life.

In Proverbs 11:2 we read,

*"When pride comes, then comes shame; But with the humble is wisdom."*

If your behavior causes shame, it is a good indication that you are carrying around some pride in your life. Once again you have come to believe that it is all right for you to behave a certain way. You might think that you are above accountability. By the way, this is exactly the reason why we have so many high-profile people in the news. They have bought the lie that they are superior and more important than others and therefore can do whatever they like.

In Proverbs 13:10 we read,

*"By pride comes nothing but strife, But with the well-advised is wisdom."*

In Proverbs 28:25 we read,

*"He who is of a proud heart stirs up strife, But he who trusts in the LORD will be prospered."*

If you leave a wake of strife wherever you go, there just may be some PRIDE in your life. If you have to argue with everyone you meet, or you are under the impression that other people are so dumb, and you are so smart, and you are always in boxing bouts with them – you have a pride issue!

Jesus made it clear that pride comes from an evil heart. In Mark 7:22 we read,

*"thefts, covetousness, wickedness, deceit, lewdness, an evil eye, blasphemy, **pride**, foolishness."*

4. Acknowledge your dependence upon God.

Turn in your Bible to the Beatitudes – they are found in Matthew 5. I want us to take a look at verse 3. We read,

*"Blessed are the poor in spirit, For theirs is the kingdom of heaven."*

Simply put, this verse tells us that a truly happy person is one who in humility acknowledges his/her need for God in their life! The person who receives Jesus Christ as Savior has publicly professed that they cannot do life apart from God.

The world says that "Christianity is a crutch", or that "Christianity is for weak-minded people." No, the truth is that those who have acknowledged God have actually humbled themselves before the Creator of all things! We are cosmic dust in comparison to the universe, but in humility, God has taken interest in us. How totally awesome is that!!!

We overcome pride by acknowledging that we are NOT "God" or "gods".

I love the great verse found in the book of Micah. It reads,

*"He has shown you, O man, what is good; And what does the LORD require of you But to do justly, To love mercy, **And to walk humbly with your God**"* (Micah 6:8)

This brings us to the final way to overcome pride.

5. Walk in humility.

None of us are better than others because of our place of birth, or position of birth, nor because of our level of education. We are not better than others because of our looks (appearance), or because of our worldly success. It has nothing to do with reputation or riches, and nothing to do with social class (i.e., rank).

Paul wrote to the Romans,

*"For I say, through the grace given to me, to everyone who is among you, not to think of himself more highly than he ought to think, but to think soberly, as God has dealt to each one a measure of faith."* (Romans 12:3)

To the Philippian church, he wrote,

*"Let nothing be done through selfish ambition or conceit, but in lowliness of mind let each esteem others better than himself. Let each of you look out not only for his own interests, but also for the interests of others."* (Philippians 2:3-4)

The best way I have ever heard Christianity presented has been in the following words, "One beggar telling another beggar where to find bread."

Jesus taught that true greatness is through SERVICE. Jesus also demonstrated SERVICE before us when he picked up the basin and the towel and began to wash His disciples' feet (John 13). Humility is when we are willing to pick up the basin and the towel and wash people's feet.

If we haven't reached this point where we can joyfully serve others, then we probably are not walking in humility. James wrote,

*"Humble yourselves in the sight of the Lord,"* (James 4:10a)

Walking in humility is a choice we must make, and it is a choice we must make daily.

## Wrap Up

Remember, there is nothing wrong with being proud of accomplishments and personal achievements in life – we are designed to enjoy setting goals and reaching them. However, haughty eyes, being PROUD, well, that is a different story. When we believe that we are better than others we have stepped over into that which God hates. The truth be known all of us have experienced being on the receiving end of a person full of pride – it was very uncomfortable. Therefore, we must guard against pride in our own lives.

I also challenge us to watch out for pride because one will begin to assume that they can do life without God or, worse yet, one will become a god unto themselves, and they may even believe that people should worship the ground they walk on. Pride will leave them trying to live life in their own strength and power. "No need for God" is their motto.

For Lucifer, it was all about "I" – this is one sure sign that you have PRIDE in your life. Is it always about YOU? Is every conversation about you, and are you always saying, "I"? Pride was what led to him being cast out of heaven, from the presence of God, and PRIDE will keep many people out of the presence of God in the future. They believe that they don't need the grace of God. PRIDE will send people to hell.

Understand that where there is pride in the Scripture, it was judged. I provided you with a whole list of examples. Pride will also be judged. The Bible says, *"and be sure your sin will find you out."* (Numbers 32:23). Therefore, we must humble ourselves before Almighty God (James 4:10). We must take the necessary steps to keep our lives free from PRIDE, and when it rears its ugly head we must quickly deal with it in a biblical fashion.

We must stand constant guard against PRIDE. It was the downfall of the devil, and he will seek for it to be our downfall as well.

- Keep your attitude in check.
- Don't revel in your press reports.
- Behave properly as a follower of Jesus Christ.
- Be utterly dependent upon God.
- Walk in humility – just a beggar telling other beggars where to find bread.

# CHAPTER 3
# A LYING TONGUE

A s followers of Jesus Christ, we are to hate the things that God hates, and we are to love the things that God loves.

In Proverbs 6:16-17 we discover the second thing that the LORD hates,

*"These six things the Lord hates, Yes, seven are an abomination to Him: A proud look, A lying tongue, Hands that shed innocent blood,"*

The LORD hates a lying tongue, and you and I are to hate (detest, abhor) a lying tongue. Once again, in the margin of your own Bible, I want you to write the word: "Lying".

In the book, *The Day America Told the Truth*, it says that 91 percent of those surveyed lie routinely about matters they consider trivial, and 36 percent lie about important matters; 86 percent lie regularly to parents, 75 percent to friends, 73 percent to siblings, and 69 percent to spouses.

The dictionary defines a lie like this: A lie is an utterance by speech or act of that which is false, with intent to mislead or delude.[1]

David wrote,

*"I said in my haste, All men are liars."* (Psalm 116:11)

One guy said that he has spent a lot of time thinking about David's statement, and he has spent a lot of time watching and listening to people, and that he is in total agreement with David.

Lies, liar, and lying – what does the GOOD BOOK have to say about the topic before us? First and foremost, without a doubt, God hates lying! Second, and just as important, we discover that lying is always viewed as wrong and evil in the Scripture. Finally, the answer to lies, being a liar, and lying is TRUTHFULNESS.

Years ago someone asked, "When is a liar no longer a liar?" The response was, "When he stops lying." WRONG! It's not when he stops lying – it is when he begins to tell the TRUTH! A liar is no longer a liar when he begins to speak TRUTH.

Now, with that as an introduction, let's take a look at what the Scripture teaches on this topic before us.

## I. The First Lie – Genesis 3:1-14

In the Bible, we have the account of Creation in Genesis 1-2, and in the third chapter, we have the entrance of sin into the world. Please take a moment and write the word "sin" somewhere on your notes. Now I want you to circle the middle letter in "sin". Again, like pride, it is the letter "I". Sin always begins where God is left out! When we set aside God and God's Word, we can count on allowing sin an entrance.

Here in the text, the serpent (the devil) is presented as the most cunning (deceiving) beast of the field. He came and he spoke to the woman (Eve), and he got her to question, to doubt what God had said to her and Adam. His words are found in verse 4,

*⁴ Then the serpent said to the woman, "You will not surely die.*

**Don't miss this** – The serpent lied to her!

What had God originally said to Adam and Eve? Turn back to Genesis 2:15-17; we read,

*"15 Then the Lord God took the man and put him in the garden of Eden to tend and keep it. 16 And the Lord God commanded the man, saying, "Of every tree of the garden you may freely eat; 17but of the tree of the knowledge of good and evil you shall not eat, for in the day that you eat of it you shall surely die."*

Think this passage through with me. The Scriptures begin with a wonderful account of creation, and then tragedy hits – the first couple God created believes a lie, and then forgets what God said, and then what follows is the culmination of the ruination of man by that lie.

Do we ever really consider that the mess we are presently living in is because of the sin of lying? Everything about the FALL of mankind started with a lie. Just thinking about that ought to cause us to HATE lying!

## II. Additional Lies – Genesis, Exodus, Joshua, Acts

Are you aware that many people build an entire doctrine on lying based on the lies that I am going to present to you in this lesson? Two examples that I am going to share with you are extremely clear that lying is just downright wrong and evil (first and last examples), and two examples that we are going to look at together are often used by pundits who believe that not all lies are wrong, and that telling "little white lies" is allowed (these will be the two middle examples).

How many of you have heard people talk about "little white lies?" Well, Austin O'Malley writes, "Those who believe that it is all right to tell little white lies soon go colorblind."

I personally hold to the belief that there is no such thing as "little white lies". A lie is a lie is a lie!

As we approach the Scripture we are going to discover that there is quite a long list of people who lied. However, I am only going to point out a short list of liars. If you want to view the long list, take a look at the footnotes at the end of this chapter. There I provide a list of many additional examples.[2]

The four examples of lying that I want us to take a look at. They are in sequential order as found in the Bible. We have already seen where the first lie was mentioned in Scripture, but where do we find the lies that followed?

A. Jacob the Deceiver – Genesis 27:22-36

The name Jacob means supplanter or deceiver. As you study the life of Jacob you discover that he lived out the meaning of his name. He deceived his father to receive the family blessing which should have gone to the firstborn (Genesis 27:22-30, 35-36). It is important for us to know that God never commended Jacob for his actions, but he did allow him time to repent, and when he did God transformed Jacob's character, but only after he repented (Genesis 39:6-11, 22-30).

By the way, Jacob's lying was the cause of a history of trouble with his brother's offspring, the Edomites. Lying has the potential to cause a lifetime of trouble.

B. The Hebrew Midwives – Exodus 1:15-21

A second example of lying found in the Bible is that of the Hebrew midwives. Turn in your Bible to Exodus 1:15-21; we read,

*15 Then the king of Egypt spoke to the Hebrew midwives, of whom the name of one was Shiphrah and the name of the other Puah; 16and he said, "When you do the duties of a midwife for the Hebrew women, and see them on the birthstools, if it is a son, then you shall kill him; but if it is a daughter, then she shall live." 17 But the midwives feared God, and did not do as the king of Egypt commanded them, but saved the male children alive. 18 So the king of Egypt called for the midwives and said to them,*

*"Why have you done this thing, and saved the male children alive?"* <u>*19*</u> <u>*And the midwives said to Pharaoh, "Because the Hebrew women are not*</u> <u>*like the Egyptian women; for they are lively and give birth before the*</u> <u>*midwives come to them."*</u> *20 Therefore God dealt well with the midwives, and the people multiplied and grew very mighty. 21 And so it was, because the midwives feared God, that He provided households for them.*

What is so odd today in Christianity is that many seek to find "proof texts" to justify lying, and they will use this example before us to try to prove their point. They will say something like, "Well, the Hebrew midwives lied to Pharaoh and God blessed them abundantly with households."

The idea that it is okay to tell lies is NOT what this passage is teaching. There are two ways for people to interpret Scripture. The first and proper way is called *Exegesis*. This word is defined as *"reading out of the scripture."* The second, and improper way to interpret Scripture is called *Isogesis*, and it is defined as *"reading into the scripture."* May I say that there are too many people today who read into the Scripture what is NOT there so that they can justify certain types of behavior traits? I mean, can you imagine people trying to justify lying because they come across people who lied in the Bible?

C. Rahab the Harlot – Joshua 2:1-24

Israel was about to cross the Jordan River and come into the Promised Land. The first obstacle other than the river was the city of Jericho. Joshua sent spies into the land, and they went to the house of a prostitute for protection. Who was this harlot? Her name was Rahab. It has been said that "Rahab was a harlot by profession and a liar by practice." I believe the spies went to Rahab's home because it would have been the last place soldiers would have looked for Hebrew spies; after all, the God of Israel didn't smile at sexual immorality. But as things often go, the spies had been seen going into Rehab's home, and it was reported to the soldiers of Jericho. They came knocking on her door, looking for the men of Israel – the spies that had come into their city. In this account we discover that Rahab lied to the soldiers – she said,

*"And the king of Jericho sent unto Rahab, saying, Bring forth the men that are come to thee, that are entered into thy house; for they are come to search out all the land. And the woman took the two men, and hid them; and she said, Yea, the men came unto me, but I knew not whence they were: and it came to pass about the time of the shutting of the gate, when it was dark, that the men went out; whither the men went I know not: pursue after them quickly; for ye will overtake them."* (Joshua 2:3-5)

I remind us not to build a doctrine about lying on this account. Some have the idea that, because Rahab lied, it is okay for us to lie. Rahab was a harlot, and she was a pagan who lived in a very idolatrous city. She was doing what she always did – lying! It's natural for people who do not know God to lie!

Something that we need to see is that Rahab recognized that the God of Israel was greater than all the pagan deities of Canaan. The gods of Canaan couldn't compare to all that she heard about what the God of Israel did for His people. Rahab was ready to receive the God of Israel, and she asked the spies to remember her and her family. What we see here is Rahab's faith. It is important for us to remember when we read about Rahab in the New Testament that she is being commended for her faith, not her lying!

Again the Bible says,

*"By faith Rahab the harlot perished not with them that were disobedient, having received the spies with peace."*

Nowhere in the Bible does it state that lying is an option or that it is okay to lie under certain situations. No, lying is always seen as a negative – always!

D. Ananias and Sapphira – Acts 5:1-11

In Acts 5 we read about another lie. We will be looking at verses 1-11 together.

In this section of Scripture, we have a couple, a husband and wife team, who conspired together to lie to Peter (an apostle); and to the entire church. They owned a piece of property and they agreed to sell it and to give the money to the apostles to distribute it among those who had need. However, what they decided was to make themselves appear better in the sight of others than they really were (that is what lying does). They agreed to sell their piece of land and give the money, but in so doing hold back a portion, telling everyone that they gave the full amount of the selling price.

Now, understand they could have given what they wanted, and they could have kept what they wanted, but they contrived a lie. They lied to Peter and to the whole church. Listen to what Peter said to Ananias,

*"But Peter said, "Ananias, why has Satan filled your heart to lie to the Holy Spirit and keep back part of the price of the land for yourself?"* (Acts 5:3)

What we must understand is that **all lying is lying to God**! Why can I say this? **Because all sin is a sin against God!** This sin was so wicked that both Ananias and Sapphira's lives were snuffed out! This demonstrates to us just how much God hates lying. They were severely judged by DEATH!

**III. What the Bible Teaches About the Sin of Lying.**

As I was writing this chapter I discovered that some sixty times, in the four Gospels alone, Jesus said, *"I tell you the truth."* In 1 Corinthians 13:6, it tells us that love (real, biblical, godly love) rejoices in the truth. In Jesus' high priestly prayer He prayed, *"Sanctify them* (disciples) *by thy truth, your word is truth."*

The focus of the Christian ought to always be on the truth. This is the opposite of lies and lying – being true and being truthful. As followers of Jesus Christ, we are to speak the truth.

Read carefully this wide selection of Bible verses found throughout both the Old and New Testaments. Repetition is important - it is how we learn.

A. Exodus 20:16 (from the Ten Commandments).

In Exodus 20, that passage where we find the Ten Commandments, we read,

*You shall not bear false witness against your neighbor.* (Exodus 20:16)

B. Leviticus 19:11 (a part of the Moral Laws of God).

*You shall not steal, nor deal falsely, nor lie to one another.*

Follower of Jesus – I challenge you to look at the LAWS found here in Leviticus. You will discover that they fall into different classifications – moral, ceremonial, civic, and so forth. However, what you will discover is that MORAL LAW crosses all generational boundaries and is applicable to all of God's people. Such is the case with what we read here in Lev. 19:11 concerning lying. Plainly put we are NOT to lie to one another. This crosses into every culture and every nation of people.

C. Proverbs 6:16-17 (God hates lying).

*These six things the Lord hates, Yes, seven are an abomination to Him: A proud look, A lying tongue, Hands that shed innocent blood,*

D. Psalm 120:2 (the Psalmist desired to be delivered).

Consider the prayer of the Psalmist,

*"Deliver my soul, O LORD, from lying lips And from a deceitful tongue."* (Psalm 120:2)

E. John 8:44 (who are you most like?).

*"You are of your father the devil, and the desires of your father you want to do. He was a murderer from the beginning, and does not stand in the truth, because there is no truth in him. When he speaks a lie, he*

*speaks from his own resources, for he is a liar and the father of it."* (John 8:44)

According to John 8, the devil is a liar and the father of all lies (John 8:44). I tell people all the time that we are no more like God than when we speak **TRUTH,** and no more like the devil than when we speak LIES. He is a LIAR and the father of it!

F. Colossians 3:9 (like soiled clothes we are to put off lying).

When we became Christians there were certain things that we were to put off – as if they were soiled clothes (dirty clothes). Paul writes,

*"Lie not one to another, seeing that ye have put off the old man with his deeds;"* (Colossians 3:9)

G. Ephesians 4:25 (put it completely away).

Paul also penned the following words (under the inspiration of the Holy Spirit),

*"Therefore, putting away lying, "Let each one of you speak truth with his neighbor," for we are members of one another."* (Ephesians 4:25)

H. Revelation 21:8 (all liars will ultimately be judged).

*"...all liars shall have their part in the lake which burns with fire and brimstone, which is the second death."*

As the Bible closes, we have a picture of Paradise, into which are gathered the lovers and doers of truth, and from which is excluded "everyone that loves and practices a lie". The ultimate judgment upon liars is hell fire. The Bible is clear that *"all liars"* are to have their part *"in the lake that burns with fire and brimstone; which is the second death."*

The Bible is never okay with lying under any circumstances. Lying is always pictured as wrong and evil. God hates it, and so should we. As born-again believers, we ought to be different, and the difference ought to show up in that we speak the truth.

**IV. It Is Decision Time (what will you do?)**

What will be your character? Will you be a person of **TRUTH** or a person who **lies**? Will you accept that it is all right to lie under certain situations, or will you be a person who holds to the principles found in the Bible? Will you hold firmly to the fact that God is a God of TRUTH and, therefore, His followers are also to be people of TRUTH.

## Liars or Truth Tellers

There is a very interesting verse found in the book of Titus that reads,

*"One of them, a prophet of their own, said, "<u>Cretans are always liars</u>, evil beasts, lazy gluttons."* (Titus 1:12)

Can you imagine history recording that the people on the Island of Crete were *"always liars"*? Do you know how people become *"always liars"*? They practice lying!

Remember that I asked you the question: When is a liar no longer a liar? It is not when they stop lying, but when they start to tell the truth. As followers of Jesus, we are called to be truth-tellers!

John the beloved disciple wrote,

*"I have no greater joy than to hear that my children <u>walk in truth</u>."* (3 John 4)

Jesus said,

*"And you shall know the truth, and the truth shall make you free."* (John 8:32)

What sets people free? Truth!

The Gospel message is a message of truth. Truth sets people free! Let us, therefore, be people who speak the truth!

## Wrap Up

Our text has been direct and very clear. God hates lying, and you and I should hate lying as well. What truth do we need to keep in mind as believers? Here are five truths that we have looked at throughout this study. They are:

1. Satan was the first liar – he is the father of all lies (John 8:44).
2. Sin is the result of believing a lie (Genesis 3).
3. People in the Bible lied, but God NEVER justified their lies.
4. Throughout the Scripture, lying is condemned, and ultimately the habitual (unsaved) liar will have their place in the lake of fire.
5. Now is decision time – commit yourself to speak TRUTH. Do not lie to one another.

End Notes:

[1] Henry Clay Trumbull, A Lie Is Never Justified, an Online book

[2] Satan – Gen. 3:4, Cain – Gen. 4:9, Sarah – Gen. 18:15, Jacob – Gen. 27:19, Joseph's brethren – Gen. 37:31-32, Gibeonites – Joshua 9:9-13, Samson – Judges 16:10, Saul – I Sam. 15:13, Michal – I Sam. 19:14, David – I Sam. 21:2, Prophets of Bethel – I Kings 13:18, Gehazi – II Kings 5:22, Job's friends – Job 13:4, Ninevites – Nah. 3:1, Peter – Matt. 26:72, Ananias – Acts 5:5, Cretans – Titus 1:12

# CHAPTER 4
# HANDS THAT SHED INNOCENT BLOOD

I nnocent people are dying in record numbers throughout our country, and around the world. As I type this chapter, Russia has invaded Ukraine and many innocent people are being killed. War really has no winners. But war isn't the only way that people are being killed. Consider the following examples:

- Serial Killers

Serial killers suffer from Antisocial Personality Disorder and appear normal or charming, sometimes referred to as the "*mask of sanity.*"

The term *serial killer* was coined in the 1970s due to cases such as Ted Bundy and David Berkowitz.

According to an FBI Behavioral Unit study, 85% of the world's serial killers are in America. At any given time, 20 - 50 unidentified, active serial killers are at work, continually changing their targets and methods.[1]

- Violent Crime in America

The CDC reported that in the United States of America over 26,031 people were murdered in 2022.

Several years ago in Moscow, Idaho, 22-year-old Katy Benoit, a student at the University of Idaho, was shot and killed by a former UI professor. Apparently the student and professor were seeing one another, and the relationship ended. The professor shot Katy and later was found dead in a Moscow hotel with a gunshot to the head.

And there we have another violent crime in America – this time close to home.

• Spousal Abuse and Death –

Every 4 hours in this country a woman is killed by her domestic partner.

A bus stop billboard with a picture of a casket with flowers on top read, "He beat her 150 times… she got flowers once."

• Abortion (An Industry of Death) –

Abortion is taking the life of an innocent baby.

Are you aware that 18 days after conception the heart beats on its own? At 6 weeks the baby quickly moves in the womb. Brain waves are present at 8 weeks and the child grabs and swims freely, the heartbeat is measurable. At 12 weeks the baby cries, sucks its thumb, sleeps, and wakes. All organs and systems function, including mental. The unborn infant can definitely feel pain. From this point on nothing new develops, there is just growth and a maturing process.

Nearly one in four pregnancies in the United States ends in abortion.

About 1.7 million abortions are done annually, with nearly one-eighth during the second or third trimester. Ninety-three percent of the time, there is no "special case"--a mother whose life is threatened, a rape or incest victim, or a child with predictions of health problems. (William Bennett)

I had a woman who used to attend church here say to me, "You just don't understand. I had an abortion because I was too young to take care of a baby. I'm glad that that was an option for me."

## NEWS FLASH

If you are too young to care for a baby, you are too young to be having sex! Sex produces babies! An evil decision should not be based on a sinful decision!

One pregnant woman said, "In this society we save whales, we save timber wolves and bald eagles and Coke bottles. Yet, everyone wanted me to throw away my baby."

My friend, you and I are living in a society where innocent people are being murdered every day. The death of innocent people is something that God hates, and you and I are to hate it too.

Our text before us says,

*"These six things the Lord hates, Yes, seven are an abomination to Him: A proud look, A lying tongue, Hands that shed innocent blood,"* (Proverbs 6:16-17)

Write in the margin of your Bible the word: "Murder".

How are we to understand all of this today? Well, again, I believe that we need to turn to the Bible for our understanding. We also need to allow Scripture to dictate to us how we are going to respond biblically to the shedding of innocent blood. As followers of Jesus Christ, we need to develop a Biblical Worldview. The Bible must be our guide for how we handle this whole idea of *"hands that shed innocent blood"*.

First, I believe we need to know that not all deaths are murder. The Bible speaks of accidental death.

## I. Accidental Death (Unintentional Death)

There is a huge difference between accidental death and intentional murder. I would even say that there is a big difference between premeditated murder and fits of rage. How should Christians respond to someone who accidentally kills another person? What should be the punishment, if any? Well, again, we must search the Scripture – the Bible provides for us the answers!

A. Horns of the Altar – Exodus 21:12-14, I Kings 2:28-29

It is interesting that in the Bible horns are a picture of judgment, and of power, but they also were used as a place of sanctuary.

In Exodus 21:12–14 the LORD said,

*"Anyone who strikes a man and kills him shall surely be put to death. However, if he does not do it intentionally, but God lets it happen, he is to flee to a place I will designate. If a man schemes and kills another man deliberately, take him away from my altar and put him to death."*

Prior to the establishment of the cities of refuge, temporary safety could be gained by fleeing to a sanctuary and grasping the horns of the altar. Once there, a Levitical tribunal would then decide the person's fate.

In I Kings, chapter 1, there is the account where Adonijah, the half-brother of Solomon, sought to make himself king of Israel. When things didn't work out for him, and King David proclaimed his son Solomon the next king of Israel, we discover that Adonijah went into the sanctuary, where he took hold of the *"horns of the altar"* (1:50). He was seeking refuge. Solomon had him taken and brought into his presence, and sent him to his house.

## Adonijah Was Put to Death

When we come to I Kings 2, we discover that Adonijah went to Bathsheba, requesting that she ask Solomon to give Abishag the Shunamite to him as his wife. When Bathsheba made the request Solomon saw it as another way in which Adonijah was seeking to squeeze himself into the position of being king. Solomon had Adonijah put to death.

## Abiathar the Priest Removed from Office

As we further make our way through this second chapter we discover that those who had aligned themselves with Adonijah were fearful. Solomon called for Abiathar the priest, and removed him from serving as a priest. He sent him to Anathoth to live out the remaining years of his life.

## Joab the Defector put to Death

Joab, who was a very successful general in David's army, later defected to the side of Adonijah and supported him. When he also received the news that Solomon had put to death Adonijah and removed Abiathar the priest, he became fearful, and he fled to the tabernacle where he grabbed hold of the horns of the altar and held on dearly. He was seeking sanctuary.

Look at verse 28, and to the end of the chapter…

*"Then news came to Joab, for Joab had defected to Adonijah, though he had not defected to Absalom. So Joab fled to the tabernacle of the Lord, and took hold of the horns of the altar. And King Solomon was told, "Joab has fled to the tabernacle of the Lord; there he is, by the altar." Then Solomon sent Benaiah the son of Jehoiada, saying, "Go, strike him down." So Benaiah went to the tabernacle of the Lord, and said to him, "Thus says the king, 'Come out!' " And he said, "No, but I will die here." And Benaiah brought back word to the king, saying, "Thus said Joab, and thus*

*he answered me." Then the king said to him, "<u>Do as he has said, and</u> <u>strike him down and bury him, that you may take away from me and from</u> <u>the house of my father the innocent blood which Joab shed.</u> So the Lord will return his blood on his head, because he struck down two men more right- eous and better than he, and killed them with the sword— Abner the son of Ner, the commander of the army of Israel, and Amasa the son of Jether, the commander of the army of Judah—though my father David did not know it. Their blood shall therefore return upon the head of Joab and upon the head of his descendants forever. But upon David and his descendants, upon his house and his throne, there shall be peace forever from the Lord." So Benaiah the son of Jehoiada went up and struck and killed him; and he was buried in his own house in the wilderness. The king put Benaiah the son of Jehoiada in his place over the army."*

Joab was put to death because of his conspiracy against the king- dom, but also because of the "innocent blood" that he had shed. Blood that David the king did not know about.

Later in Israel's history when they came into the Promised Land God had designated cities of refuge for a person who killed someone accidentally (Numbers 35:15–32).

Let's turn our attention to these cities now.

B. Cities of Refuge – Exodus 21:12-14; Numbers 35:6-34; Deuteronomy 19:1-13; Joshua 20:1-9

In the Old Testament, we find four key passages telling us about the cities of refuge. These passages give us insight into the right to asylum and the sanctuary provided by these cities. Take the time needed to read through the following passages of Scripture listed above. Each speaks about the cities of refuge.

The Hebrew meaning of *"city of refuge"* can be translated as "a city of intaking." It is important for us to understand that sanctuary was offered before the settlement of the Promised Land, but that it was only available to the one charged with accidental manslaughter.

In Exodus 21:12-13, we read,

*"He who strikes a man so that he dies shall surely be put to death. However, if he did not lie in wait, but God delivered him into his hand, then I will appoint for you a place where he may flee."*

A key passage dealing with the cities of refuge is found in Joshua 20. I would suggest that you take a moment and read through that passage of Scripture and then come back to this book.

### The Locations of the Cities of Refuge

In Joshua 20:7-8, we read that Moses was commanded to establish six cities of refuge. Take a look at a Biblical map to find these cities. Three were located on each side of the Jordan River:

- In the East were: **Bezer** in the territory of the Reubenites, **Ramoth** in Gilead, and **Golan** in the area of Bashan (Deut. 4:43).
- On the West side of the Jordan were **Kedesh** in Galilee, **Shechem** in Ephraim, and **Kirjath-arba** or Hebron in the hill country of Judah

### The Importance of the Cities of Refuge

These six cities were located in strategic areas on both sides of the Jordan so that a city was easily reachable by a person responsible for an accidental homicide. The person needed to find sanctuary immediately because a member of the dead man's family would pursue him. This person was called, "the avenger of blood", and they sought to kill the slayer of their kin for the harm done to the family or clan.

### Blood Feud

Have heard of the Hatfields and the McCoys? Well, an interesting bit of insight into Israel's early history reveals that before the development of the cities of refuge, an accidental death could result in a blood feud that terminated only with the extinction of one family. The establishment of the cities of refuge served a humanitarian purpose by transforming a case of homicide from a private feud between two families to a judicial matter settled by a group of elders.[2]

## Requirements to Enter the City of Refuge

The requirements to enter a city of refugee are found in Numbers 35. They are as follows:

1. The death must have occurred by accident without premeditation or intent (see Numbers 35:16–18, 20–23).

If it was concluded that the death was an accident, the avenger of blood could not put to death the person who accidentally killed their kin.

2. The manslayer, once admitted to the city, could not leave until the death of the high priest (Numbers 35:25; Joshua. 20:6).

If he chose to leave the city before that time, he could be killed by the avenger of blood (Numbers 35:26–28). However, after the death of the high priest, the manslayer could return to his home and family.

According to Numbers 35:15, the sanctuary was not limited to the people of Israel, but was extended to the stranger and sojourner among them.

Next, let's turn our attention to premeditated murder. What does the Bible say on this subject matter?

## II. Premeditated Murder

As we read through the Bible, we do find people who actually planned to kill someone – this is called premeditated murder. Most murder victims are innocent. Remember, God hates *"hands that shed innocent blood."*

Let's take a look at four examples from the Scripture of those who actually planned out their murderous actions.

A. Cain planned to kill Abel – Genesis 4:8 (The First Murder)

Here we have before us the first murder in the Bible. It is when Cain rose up against his brother, Abel, and killed him. We read here, in Genesis 4:8, the following words –

*"Now Cain talked with Abel his brother; and it came to pass, when they were in the field, that Cain rose up against Abel his brother and killed him."*

As I read this verse, it appears to me that it was premeditated murder. Cain had talked with his brother Abel, and later (it came to pass) when they were in the field together he rose up and killed him.

This happened long before the Law was given, or the Cities of Refuge were established. However, Cain did not go unpunished for his crime. In Genesis 4:9-15,

*"Then the Lord said to Cain, "Where is Abel your brother?" He said, "I do not know. Am I my brother's keeper?" And He said, "What have you done? The voice of your brother's blood cries out to Me from the ground. So now you are cursed from the earth, which has opened its mouth to receive your brother's blood from your hand. When you till the ground, it shall no longer yield its strength to you. A fugitive and a vagabond you shall be on the earth." And Cain said to the Lord, "My punishment is greater than I can bear! Surely You have driven me out this day from the face of the ground; I shall be hidden from Your face; I shall be a fugitive and a vagabond on the earth, and it will happen that anyone who finds me*

*will kill me." And the Lord said to him, "Therefore, whoever kills Cain, vengeance shall be taken on him sevenfold."* <u>*And the Lord set a mark on Cain, lest anyone finding him should kill him."*</u>

What was Cain's three-fold punishment?

1. The ground would no longer yield its strength to him.
2. He would be a perpetual fugitive and vagabond.
3. God placed a mark on Cain so that people would not kill him.

Cain was going to have a miserable rest of his earthly life.

The point that I want to make is that Cain killed innocent blood when he killed his brother, Abel.

B. Saul planned to have David killed – 1 Samuel 19:1-24

The first King of Israel began his reign in humility, but later he allowed pride to go to his head. He saw David praised by the people he ruled over, and he began to despise him. Saul became bent on destroying David (v. 1). However, Saul's son Jonathan loved David, and understood that David was a good man. He and David were BFFs! Jonathan pleaded with his father not to seek to put David to death. Listen to Jonathan's words in I Samuel 19:5,

*"For he took his life in his hands and killed the Philistine, and the Lord brought about a great deliverance for all Israel. You saw it and rejoiced.* <u>*Why then will you sin against innocent blood, to kill David without a cause?"*</u>

Jonathan knew that if his father succeed in killing David he would be taking an innocent life.

As you read through this account you discover that Saul told his son that he wouldn't harm David. David was allowed to come into Saul's presence, but while they were dining Saul picked up a spear and threw it at David, seeking to pin him to the wall (v. 10). David escaped that night. Saul sent soldiers looking for David. He wanted them to bring David back to him so that he could put him to death (v. 15). David escaped and went to Samuel at Ramah.

Throughout Saul's career as King of Israel, he was jealous of David, and he sought to shed innocent blood.

C. David's men planned the killing of Ishbosheth – 2 Samuel 4:5-12

There is a third example of men shedding innocent blood in the Old Testament. Two men by the names of Rimmon and Rechab sought to protect David by killing a member of Saul's household. They saw him as an enemy of David. These men came into the house of Ishbosheth and killed him while he was sleeping on his bed. They cut off his head and brought it to David. David was not pleased and told them that they had killed an innocent man. David had these men executed for their crime of stabbing to death an innocent man.

God HATES those who murder, and who take the lives of innocent people. You and I ought to HATE what God hates.

D. Jezebel planned the killing of Naboth – 1 Kings 21:1-29

Are we aware of how many people are murdered for the things they possess? People are murdered for their possessions. People have killed others for shoes, clothing, and watches here in America. What a sick society when material things become more valuable than human life!

In I Kings 21 we have the account where Ahab's wife, the wicked Jezebel, hears her husband crying because he can't possess his neighbor's vineyard, which is situated next to his palace. He wanted to turn the vineyard into a vegetable garden. He offered to trade it or buy it, but Naboth the owner didn't want to sell it because it was a part of his inheritance.

Ahab went home and was all upset over the fact that Naboth would not even consider giving up his vineyard. He was sullen and displeased, and he went in and lay on his bed, with his face turned (pouting), and he would not eat.

Later his wicked wife Jezebel (I call her the snake) came in and saw him and asked him why he was so sullen, and why he wasn't eating. He explained to her about Naboth's vineyard, and how he sought to attain it through trade or purchase, but Naboth would not sell his father's inheritance.

Jezebel listened and then reminded her husband that he was the king of Israel and that he possessed authority. She told him to arise, eat, and that she would give him Naboth's vineyard (v. 7).

Let's see what she did -

1. She contrived a plan – v. 8-10
2. She allowed others to carry it out – v. 11-13
3. She murdered an innocent man – v. 14

Take a look at verse 14. We read,

*"Then they sent to Jezebel, saying, "Naboth has been stoned and is dead."*

The king and the queen of Israel were quick to shed innocent blood. Jezebel came and told Ahab that Naboth had been stoned to death and that he could go and possess the vineyard. Ahab got up and went to take possession of the vineyard.

I don't have the time to develop this entire story, but I do want us to see that God will always judge those who shed innocent blood. As Ahab was traveling to take possession of the vineyard he was met by Elijah, the prophet of God. Take a look at verses 19 and 23-24. We read,

- Verse 19 – *"You shall speak to him, saying, 'Thus says the Lord: "Have you murdered and also taken possession?" ' And you shall speak to him, saying, 'Thus says the Lord: "In the place where dogs licked the blood of Naboth, dogs shall lick your blood, even yours."*

- Verses 23-24 - *"And concerning Jezebel the Lord also spoke, saying, 'The dogs shall eat Jezebel by the wall of Jezreel.' The dogs shall eat whoever belongs to Ahab and dies in the city, and the birds of the air shall eat whoever dies in the field."*

Finally, how are we to respond to those who shed innocent blood? What does the Bible say?

### III. God's Solution (What do we do?)

It is very important as followers of Jesus Christ to know our Bible well, and to learn to interpret it accurately (2 Timothy 2:15). How are we as a society to handle accidental deaths? What should happen to those who plan out their violent acts of premeditated murders? The actions of individual Christians and society as a whole are extremely important! The best response is always a BIBLICAL response! We must always look to God and His Word. God has provided us with everything we need for faith and practice. We have 66 books in the Bible to guide us (Genesis to Revelation).

I want us to first take a look at why it is wrong to murder. Next, what should be done to the murderer? Finally, we need to fully be cognitive that Christians are never to be guilty of murder. Let's look at this in that order.

A. Why is it wrong to murder?

1. Murder is wrong because we are made in God's image – Genesis 9:5-6

*"Surely for your lifeblood I will demand a reckoning; from the hand of every beast I will require it, and from the hand of man. From the hand of every man's brother I will require the life of man. "<u>Whoever sheds man's</u>*

*blood, By man his blood shall be shed; For in the image of God He made*
*man."*

Premeditated murder against the innocent is wrong and it is something that God hates. Murder is plainly wrong because mankind is
made in the image of god.

Various interpreters of the Bible believe that the location of the
'image' of God in man is found in his ability to reason, his creativ-
ity, speech, or his spiritual nature. However, it is more likely that
"image" is in reference to the whole of man, rather than some part
or aspect of him. Man is a trichotomy being (I Thessalonians 5:23).
The whole man, spirit, body, and soul, is the image of God; man is
the corporeal image (body) of the incorporeal God (Spirit). [3]

2. Murder is wrong because of the Sixth Commandment – Exodus
20:13; Deuteronomy 5:17

God's established a LAW that clearly states that murder is prohib-
ited. In Exodus 20:13 we read,

*"Thou shalt not kill (murder)."*

If we turned to the New Testament we would read Jesus' commen-
tary on the Law. Jesus taught,

*"You have heard that it was said to those of old, 'You shall not murder,*
*and whoever murders will be in danger of the judgment.'* [22] *But I say to*
*you that whoever is angry with his brother without a cause shall be in*
*danger of the judgment. And whoever says to his brother, 'Raca!' shall be*
*in danger of the council. But whoever says, 'You fool!' shall be in danger of*
*hell fire.*" (Matthew 5:21-21)

Here Jesus is expanding the Law. It's not just the act of murder; it's
the thought of murder. The thought of murder rages in the heart of
the person who allows anger to control him/her.

B. What is to be done to the murderer?

Can I tell you first what the Bible doesn't tell us to do? It doesn't tell us that we need to provide three meals a day, hot and cold running water, cable television, exercise equipment, college education, the best medical care, and sports playgrounds for those convicted of murder. Something is terribly wrong with a society that believes convicted murderers deserve to have living conditions better than the poor and middle class in America.

So, what does the Scripture teach as to what should be done with the murderer?

1. Murderers are to be put to death on the basis of witnesses – Numbers 35:19-30; Deuteronomy 17:6-12

According to the Bible, no one is to be put to death by the words of one witness. There must be the *"testimony of witnesses"* before a person can be put to death.

Deuteronomy 17 tells us that there must be two or three witnesses before a person can be put to death for murder.

When this was written, it spoke specifically about the witness of individuals. Today we have other types of witnesses, things like DNA, and photography. I believe that these things are witnesses as well.

2. Crimes of murder are to be dealt with – Deuteronomy 21:1-9

I hope that we already understand that murder is a capital offense. If a person plans a murder and kills someone, that person is to be put to death. They are to be put to death because they took the life of another human being.

In Deuteronomy 21, we read about what happens when a body is found, but no one knows whether an accident occurred or a murder. God set it up so that they would actually measure from the body to the nearest town. All the elders of the town were to bring out a heifer and offer it as a sacrifice. As they were doing this, they would wash their hands over the head of the animal saying,

*"Our hands have not shed blood, nor have our eyes seen it."* (v. 7)

This act of sacrifice and the washing of the hands provided atonement for Israel. The blood of the innocent would not be charged against them. God would put away the guilt when they did what was right.

### Other Death - Sentence Crimes

By the way – FYI – other crimes that were capital offenses in the Bible include:

- Striking a parent – Exodus 21:15
- Kidnapping – Exodus 21:16; Deuteronomy 24:7
- Cursing a parent – Exodus 21:17

C. Christians are to never suffer as a murderer – 1 Peter 4:15

*"But let none of you suffer as a murderer, a thief, an evildoer, or as a busy-body in other people's matters."*

Christians suffer, and the passage where 1 Peter 4:15 comes from shows us that Christians suffered greatly during the New Testament era. Persecution is no excuse for lawlessness. Christians are not called to retaliate – we are called to suffer as Jesus suffered. This is what separates true Christianity from those of the world.

The Greek word for *"suffer"* used here in this verse can speak of being put to death. No believer in Christ is to be put to death for murder. It goes against the very idea of Christianity and the newness of life that is provided in a relationship with Jesus Christ.

Allow me to bring all of this to a close.

### Wrap Up

God hates *"hands that shed innocent blood."* (Proverbs 6:17c).

Let us never feel sorry for the murderer – it is the innocent victim that we should have empathy for, not the criminal who has viciously killed. To take a life means that you forfeit your own!

In America, we have an epidemic of hands that are shedding innocent blood. We cannot be quiet about it as it is happening. May God raise up people who will be the VOICE for the innocent!

As followers of Jesus Christ, the Bible is our guidebook, and it teaches that if a person takes the life of another person they are to be put to death. We must hold to a strong belief in capital punishment. After all, mankind was created in the image of God.

NEVER under any circumstance legalize abortion in your mind and heart. It is taking the life of an innocent baby!

If you are too young to be a parent, you are too young to be having sex!

There is a sharp contrast between accidental death and premeditated murder. God allows protection for those who accidentally kill someone, but the one who plans out his murder, well, that person is to be put to death.

I often think of how many fewer murders we would have in the U.S. if ,instead of putting these sentenced murderers on death row, we actually carried out their sentences. I personally believe that the death sentence is a deterrent to those who think about murder.

No one ever gets away with murder - that might be a statement we use at times, but eventually, he/she will be judged. Payday will be someday for all murderers. According to Revelation 21:8, we read,

*"But the cowardly, unbelieving, abominable, murderers, sexually immoral, sorcerers, idolaters, and all liars shall have their part in the lake which burns with fire and brimstone, which is the second death."*

End Notes:

[1] http://karisable.com/crserial.htm

[2] Bible Handbook

[3] Wood, D. R. W., & Marshall, I. H. (1996). New Bible dictionary (3rd ed.) (499). Leicester, England; Downers Grove, Ill.: InterVarsity Press.

# CHAPTER 5
# A HEART THAT DEVISES WICKED PLANS

P salm 36:4 is a very insightful verse. It reads,

*"He devises wickedness on his bed; He sets himself in a way that is not good; He does not abhor evil."*

There are actually people who plot wickedness while they lie in bed. They allow evil imaginations to run wild. They are planning their next wicked deed(s). Know anyone like that, or heard of anyone doing this?

Our Scripture today is from Proverbs 6:18a,

*"A heart that devises wicked plans, Feet that are swift in running to evil,"*

I have had you write Pride, Lying, Murder, and now I want you to write, "Plotting Wickedness" in the margin of your Bible. God hates those who plan wicked deeds.

Here are some of the various ways that different translations of the Bible state this verse:

- *NLT - A heart that plots evil.*
- *NIV - A heart that devises wicked schemes.*

- *KJV - A heart that devises wicked imaginations.*
- *ASV - A heart that deviseth wicked purposes.*
- *BBE - A heart full of evil design.*

What we are looking at here are thoughts of iniquity. How ugly is the human heart at times? We can allow our hearts to think about some terrible things. It has been said, "What is played in the theatre of the mind will eventually be played out in the theatre of life." Therefore, as followers of Jesus Christ, we must HATE what God hates. We must block the wicked plans that we so often think about.

It wasn't always this way. There was a time early on in human history when mankind didn't have hearts that were plotting wicked purposes. There was a time when mankind was good, perfect, and innocent. However, it didn't last long. We are in the mess we are because of open rebellion in the heart of man. We obstinately refuse to obey the voice of God, our creator. We choose to sin, and we choose to have hearts that are bent on planning evil things. There is hope, and when I bring this chapter to a close we will look at this hope.

I want us to move through three stages. First, I want us to see what it was like at one time with innocent hearts. Next, I want us to see where and why we have fallen hearts, and finally, I want to share the hope that is available with hearts that have been redeemed.

### I. Innocent Hearts (Created that way)

When God created Adam, he was created in a state of innocence. There was no such thing as sin, no evil around him. Everything was PERFECT!

- Perfect weather all the time (it is believed that a water vapor surrounded the earth, keeping out harmful UV rays).
- Animals all lived in perfect harmony. The lion and the lamb did lie down together. The lion didn't dream of lamb chops.
- The environment was perfect; nothing was off, nothing!

- Adam and Eve were a perfect age and probably never aged. They didn't worry about cancer or age spots on their skin.
- They both had perfect health. They never saw sickness of any kind.
- They enjoyed the work God gave them to do. They liked what they did, and they liked their boss.
- They had perfect foods that filled them and satisfied them fully.

God was present, and Adam and God walked together in the cool of the Garden each night. They shared with one another – together there was perfect fellowship.

When God created for Adam his helpmeet, she, too, was perfect. She had no one to compare herself with. She was a total WOMAN! Both Adam and Eve enjoyed all that God had created for them.

We really see the innocence in the words found in Genesis 2:25,

*"And they were both naked, the man and his wife, and were not ashamed."*

Can you imagine being in a state of innocence? Can you imagine being in a perfect environment, a place void of all evil? Think for a moment of the most perfect place you have ever visited. Multiply that a million times, and you still don't have anything that comes close to what Adam and Eve had in the Garden of Eden.

I believe that I can honestly say that most people long for innocence again. Most people would love to live in an environment where there is an absence of brokenness. People desire and long for open and honest trust.

## II. Fallen Hearts (Activated in rebellion)

Genesis 3 is a pivotal chapter in the Scripture. Whenever anyone asks you why we have problems in our world, society at large, or here in our little community, all you have to do is point them to Genesis 3.

Adam and Eve had it made in the shade (literally). They enjoyed a perfect creation – void and absent of any kind of brokenness. But it didn't last long. The serpent (his names: Lucifer, Satan, and Devil) showed up, and he deceived the woman. <u>Lucifer devised a plan in his heart to deceive the couple that God had created.</u> He spoke to the woman and got her to doubt God and question God's authority in her life. He encouraged in her a desire to become *"like God"* (v. 5). And as a result, the woman partook of the forbidden tree (the tree of the knowledge of good and evil), and gave it to her husband, and together they ate of it (v. 6), and their eyes were opened, and they now knew that they were naked (v. 7). Their innocence was LOST! Their perfect state was now broken and shattered. The world they knew became a very twisted place.

Are you aware that the first religious act recorded in the Bible is the sewing of fig leaves to make coverings (v. 7)? This continues to be the mode of operation even to this day. People are always trying to COVER their nakedness before Almighty God. Religions, cults, occult, new age, and isms of all sorts are all ways for mankind to try to cover for the loss of their innocence. It is man's attempt to fix what he has broken. Adam and Eve knew that something was totally different - something was lost! What was lost? INNO-CENCE! Have you ever done something that you KNEW was wrong, and immediately afterward you had GUILT? This is prob-ably what Adam and Eve experienced for the first time ever! Can you imagine how heavy that guilt was?

Next, we find that Adam and Eve hid from the presence of God (v. 8). Is it possible to hide from an all-seeing (omnipresent) God? Absolutely not, but in their new, fallen state, they didn't know that. God was well aware of what had happened, and what his pair on the ground were doing. They weren't doing anything that God couldn't see.

God comes and calls out for Adam, *"Where are you?"* (v. 9). Can you imagine Adam and Eve hearing God's voice after the fact, after they had been disobedient to His command? Did the voice of God sound different? Take a look at what Adam says after he steps out from behind the trees. He says,

*"I heard your voice in the garden, and I was afraid because I was naked; and I hid myself."* (v. 10)

Here we find fear for the first time in the Bible. Adam was afraid (v. 10). What must that have felt like? Do you remember a time when you were really afraid? I'm not talking about carnival ride fear or roller-coaster ride fear; I'm talking about being wholly afraid!

- Have you ever done something wrong and were afraid of what your parents were going to do to you when you faced them?
- Ever do something at school and were afraid that you were going to face the principal?
- Ever got in trouble with the law and stood before a judge? Did you have fear and trepidation?

God questions Adam,

*"Who told you that you were naked? Have you eaten from the tree of which I commanded you that you should not eat?"* (v. 11)

That is a legitimate question. In his new, fallen state the first thing Adam resorts to is the blame game. It is someone else's fault. Consider how quickly Adam answers God. He says,

*"The woman whom You gave to be with me, she gave me of the tree, and I ate."* (v. 12)

Do you see how quickly, in a fallen state, where innocence is lost, a man will turn on a woman? However, Adam didn't just turn on Eve, he turned on God. Here in this verse, Adam is saying to God it is your fault that I am covered with fig leaves, and that I hid among the trees, and that I ate from the tree of the knowledge of good and evil; after all, you gave me this woman. This would have never happened to me if it wasn't for this woman. God, you are the one who is really at fault here, not me.

God looked at the woman and He asked her,

*"What is this that you have done?"* (v. 13)

Again, almost immediately the woman does the blame game, and she accuses the serpent of her rebellion against God's command. She says,

*"The serpent deceived me, and I ate."*

What Eve was saying is that it's not my fault. You can't hold me accountable. I was deceived, and it was in deception that I partook of the forbidden tree. She refused to acknowledge her open rebellion against God. She refused to confess that she completely understood the command to NOT eat off the tree of the knowledge of good and evil, but she wasn't going to go there with God. It is always someone else's fault that I sinned.

As I was studying through this passage of Scripture, I began to think that here we have before us every excuse we make even today as to why we rationalize *"A heart that devises wicked plans,"* Consider the following twelve ideas:

1. We don't appreciate what we have.

I know that Eve was deceived, but it also appears to me that neither Eve nor Adam were fully satisfied with what they possessed. They wanted more. They had no clue what the more was, but they bought the lie that God was holding out on them.

Many people have planned some wicked schemes based on the idea that God is holding back more from them. They might not be thinking that in their head, but they are in their heart.

Bernie Madoff defrauded thousands of investors of billions of dollars (18 billion is believed to be what investors lost). When I was reading about him I discovered the following line: "Madoff said he began the Ponzi scheme in the early 1990s." There we have the plotting of wicked plans. It started in Madoff's heart!

Just a few years ago I heard the story about Solyndra (Solar Panel Maker), of California's Silicon Valley, which filed Chapter 11 bankruptcy and has soaked taxpayers some 535 million dollars. (This money came from the President's stimulus package.) I bet that somewhere along the line this scheme began in someone's heart.

2. We listen to the wrong voice.

The first voice that Adam heard was the voice of God. Oh, how we need to train ourselves to hear the voice of God today. Do we KNOW when God speaks to us? God speaks through the Bible, through the Holy Spirit that dwells within the believer, through music, through other believers, and through creation. There are other ways, but that gives us some basic information.

Adam also heard the voice of Eve. Can you imagine what it was like to hear another human voice? However, the problem we have in the Genesis 3 account is that both Adam and Eve listened to the WRONG voice. Eve listened to the serpent, and Adam listened to his wife. In this case, it was deadly!

I can tell you, on the authority of God's Word, that anytime you devise wicked plans you are not listening to the voice of God.

3. We doubt and question God.

The voice she heard caused her to doubt God, and to question what God had said to her. The voice told her that God was holding out on her and Adam. The voice told her that she deserved more. So many people think they deserve more!

Are you aware that as Americans we have 80% of the world's goods, and possess 20% of the world's population? How much more do we desire?

Again, are you aware of how many evil and wicked plans are made by people who believe that God has been withholding from them? They have bought the lie that God is only trying to control them, and not that He really has a CREATOR'S CARE for them.

4. We believe that we can be God.

One of the biggest lies in the entire universe is that *"you will be like God."* This is the lie of the New Age movement, and every cult today seems to have the doctrine of demons that mankind can become a god. Because people have bought this lie many wicked imaginations have been dreamed up, and millions and millions of lives have been snuffed out by people who have believed the lie that they are gods unto themselves.

You are not god, never will be god, and never can become a god. However, you will either come to God, seek the face of God for salvation, or you will stand before God as your judge.

5. We answer to no one but ourselves.

Because people have bought the lie that they can become a god, or that they are god, they believe they answer to no one but themselves. If this is what you believe then it doesn't matter what you plan in your heart. Your heart is your guide, and whatever you plan is always right.

The Bible says,

*"There is a way that seems right to a man, But its end is the way of death."* (Proverbs 14:12)

May I remind you that the Bible tells us that we will answer to God? The Bible tells us that we are responsible to one another and that we are answerable to the laws of the land.

You are NOT an island unto yourself. You do not have a right to dwell upon wicked imaginations, developing and scheming wicked plans against others.

6. We cover up our sinful behavior and actions.

Isn't this what Adam and Eve did in their first religious act of sewing fig leaves? Many of the evil plotting people do is for the direct purpose of trying to cover their tail (pun intended).

Listen – usually, one evil imagination leads to another. There is never an end to it.

7. We believe that we can fix problems by ourselves.

Have you ever tried to fix some type of electronic item that was broken, and when you opened the case, all sorts of things fell out, and you had no idea how to put it back together? Well, this is what happened to Adam and Eve. They broke the state of innocence, and they didn't know how to fix it, but they tried.

Many times people sit up at night devising plans about how to fix things that they broke. They think about how they are going to repair fractured friendships, how they are going to get their job back, or how they are going to stop the divorce papers. What is sad is that it is often the same *"devising wicked plans"* that got them into the mess they are in in the first place.

When we try to fix things ourselves, we usually only make a greater problem.

8. We allow being afraid to control us.

How many times do we allow fear to take over all our common sense? Being afraid of what others think about us, how we are viewed, or whether we will be liked adversely affects all our thoughts and actions. We are constantly scheming plans in our hearts to make us look good and acceptable to others.

As a teenager, when I worked for the Red Lion Motor Inn, I dropped a large glass jar of olives onto the kitchen floor. It wasn't an accident, it was done out of horseplay along with a friend. I became immediately afraid that the manager of the hotel was going to walk into the kitchen, and that he was going to see what had happened. I thought my job was on the line, and my mind began racing for ways as to how I was going to explain what had happened. I jumped down from the storage area and immediately started to clean up the mess. The manager never found out, BUT my actions based on fear started to get my heart racing for ways to explain away the broken glass and spilled olives.

Being afraid and fearful will cause many of us to devise wicked plans.

9. We will blame others for our own failure.

This is what Adam and Eve both did. They were unwilling to take personal responsibility. Adam blamed God for bringing Eve into his life, and Eve blamed the serpent.

Those who scheme wicked plans are always looking for scapegoats. They are always looking for someone to take the fall for them.

Are you aware that people who have done heinous acts toward humanity have actually blamed God for their actions because he created Satan? God, you can't hold me accountable for my actions; after all, I would have never done what I did had it not been for Satan, and you created him. Therefore, you are to blame and not me.

10. We will turn on each other.

Adam quickly turned on Eve, and Eve turned on the serpent. When our hearts are full of wicked imaginations we will find it easy to turn on those who we might hold near and dear to us.

Concern for our family, friends, and neighbors means nothing when you are trying to cover your own hide.

11. We will use the ignorance card.

How many people have said, "I never knew that?" I know for a fact that everyone who drives to SLBC knows that the speed limit on

New Hampshire street is 15 miles per hour. If and when you get pulled over for going 20, you can try to use the, "I didn't know" card, but it won't work. The Spirit Lake Police have heard it before, and they will write you a ticket.

Neither Adam nor Eve was going to admit that they knew exactly what God had said to them, just maybe they didn't quite understand what it means. "Not to eat off the Tree of the Knowledge of Good and Evil." I mean, how many other possible meanings could those words have?

12. We are void of innocence and therefore we justify our actions.

We are far removed from the original Garden of Eden. Today there probably isn't one of us who wouldn't trade our present condition for that place of innocence and perfection. There is not one of us who wouldn't desire to be living in a place of perfect harmony. Can you try to comprehend being at one with God and all of our surroundings?

Because we aren't there, and we are here, in our present state of total brokenness, people's hearts plan evil designs. Nations plan wicked plots against other nations. We see this in the news almost every night.

Survival of the fittest will seek to take over. Whoever is the meanest and toughest survives, and it doesn't matter who I hurt or who gets in the way.

### III. Redeemed Hearts (Purchased by Christ)

So far we have discovered that at one time we had hearts that were innocent. The entire human race longs for that time again – and the Word of God promises us that it is coming. We also discovered that hearts became fallen, twisted, and broken when we rebelled against God. Are you aware that the first place where "*heart*" is found in the Bible is in Genesis 6:5-7, where we read why God destroyed the world with a flood? We read,

*"Then the Lord saw that the wickedness of man was great in the earth, <u>and that every intent of the thoughts of his heart was only evil continually</u>. And the Lord was sorry that He had made man on the earth, and He was grieved in His heart. So the Lord said, "I will destroy man whom I have created from the face of the earth, both man and beast, creeping thing and birds of the air, for I am sorry that I have made them."*

And the heart of mankind continues to be evil even to this day.

What we need right now are Redeemed Hearts. We need New Hearts!

Jesus taught,

*"But those things which proceed out of the mouth come from the heart, and they defile a man." For out of the heart proceed evil thoughts, murders, adulteries, fornications, thefts, false witness, blasphemies."* (Matt. 15:18-19)

The heart is the essence of who we really are. It is the CENTRALITY of our entire being! And if we were all honest right now we would readily admit that we don't like what we find in our hearts, even within the hearts of us believers. This is why David prayed,

*"Create in me a clean heart, O God, And renew a steadfast spirit within me."* (Psalm 51:10)

The prophet Jeremiah wrote,

*"The heart is deceitful above all things, And desperately wicked; Who can know it?*

Okay Pastor Kim, give us hope now. We need hope today! Please tell me that there is hope for my heart. Can I ever OVERCOME this heart problem? **Yes, we can!** There are three vital steps we need to take. There may be more, but I only want to pass along three.

1. Replace the wicked heart with a NEW heart – Ezekiel 36:26

What ALL people need today is a heart transplant. Have you ever seen a person with a sick heart? It affects their entire body. I have read that a sick heart shows up in the following areas:

### What Effects Does Heart Disease Have on the Body?

- The person affected by heart disease becomes physically inactive and suffers from constant fatigue.
- Heart disease can lead to failure in the functioning of various organs such as the liver and kidney, as well as intestines, etc.
- Blood pressure fluctuates and one suffers from either high blood pressure or low blood pressure.
- Those suffering from congenital heart disease are faced with death due to heart attacks. Oxygen supply may not be there for the brain.
- Plaque formation on the arterial walls causes coronary heart disease. The blood vessels get blocked, causing damage to various organs of the body.
- Peripheral vascular disease is due to blocked arteries in the arms and legs. It prevents the mobility of the arms and legs, causing physical disability.
- Strokes can incapacitate a person or even cause death.
- A woman with congenital heart disease can consider pregnancy but has to undergo tests and evaluation to understand the risk factors involved. There is a risk of fetal or maternal death
- Heart disease can cause depression in a person.
- A person suffering from heart disease undergoes tremendous physical and mental stress.[1]

If a sick physical heart has severe side effects on the rest of the body, then what about the sick heart of fallen mankind? A fallen heart affects the essence of who we really are! Without question, we need a Heart transplant!

God wants to provide you with a NEW HEART! Listen to this fantastic verse from the book of Ezekiel. We read,

*"A new heart also will I give you, and a new spirit will I put within you: and I will take away the stony heart out of your flesh, and I will give you an heart of flesh."* (Ezekiel 36:26)

How do we get this NEW HEART? Well, the Bible tells us,

A. We must acknowledge our wicked heart – Romans 3:23

*"For all have sinned and fall short of the glory of God."*

Did you catch the word *"all"* in that verse? No one is exempt! We all must acknowledge to God that we have hearts that *"devise wicked imagination"*.

We can't receive a new heart until we acknowledge that we have a bad heart!

B. We must believe that God wants to provide for us a New Heart – Romans 5:8

*"But God demonstrates His own love toward us, in that while we were still sinners, Christ died for us."*

A heart transplant occurs when we believe that God (our Creator) provided His Son as the answer to our heart problem. Jesus Christ died for the wickedness of our hearts. He who knew no sin became sin for us that we might become the righteousness of God in Him (2 Corinthians 5:17).

A NEW HEART is given at the moment we trust in Jesus Christ for salvation. The Bible says,

*"that Christ may dwell in your hearts through faith; that you, being rooted and grounded in love,"* (Ephesians 3:17)

C. We must call upon Jesus Christ to give us this New Heart – Romans 10:9-13 *"that if you confess with your mouth the Lord Jesus and believe in your heart that God has raised Him from the dead, you will be saved. [10] For with the heart one believes unto righteousness, and with the mouth confession is made unto salvation. For the Scripture says, "Whoever believes on Him will not be put to shame." For there is no distinction between Jew and Greek, for the same Lord over all is rich to all who call upon Him. For "whoever calls on the name of the Lord shall be saved."*

I guarantee you, based on the authority of God's Word, that if you will acknowledge your wicked heart, acknowledge that God wants to give you a New Heart, and if you will by faith (absolute trust) call upon God's Son Jesus Christ to save you, you will at that very moment be given a NEW HEART, and God's Spirit will take up residence in your heart.

How is that for hope?

If you bought a car, and the motor went bad right away, what would you do? You would have the motor replaced. This same can be said about our hearts. I submit to you that our heart is bad, and we need to go to the Master Mechanic (Jesus Christ) and have Him replace it.

God is in the business of REDEEMING the heart of mankind, and once our hearts have been radically changed, we must seek to maintain our REDEEMED hearts. This brings us to the next step.

2. Watch over your heart continually – Proverbs 4:23

*"Keep your heart with all diligence, For out of it spring the issues of life."*

Have you heard the phrase "Heart Healthy"? Well, this is what we have before us in this verse. In the same way that people seek to maintain a healthy physical heart, so we should have the same concern for our spiritual personhood (the real us). We should desire to have a healthy spiritual life. It should be a priority (the highest priority) for the believer to have a HEALTHY SPIRITUAL HEART!

The words *"Keep your heart"* tell us that we have something personally that we need to be doing. In other words, we have a responsibility in keeping our spiritual hearts healthy.

Next, consider the words, *"with all diligence"*. The word *"diligence"* here in Hebrew means, "above" or "more than all." Why do we keep our hearts? Because everything, and I do mean everything, flows from the heart. The heart is the source of whatever affects life and character (Matthew 12:35; 15:19). Therefore, do all you can to guard your heart!

How do we watch over our hearts? We watch over our spiritual heart the same way we watch over our physical heart.

- **Eat right** – We take in a good diet of heart-healthy foods. Here I am talking about what we read, listen to, watch on television and the movies, and anything else that comes into the heart.
- **Drink plenty of water** – The Scripture is called "water". We may live for anywhere between 46 and 73 days without food (not in all cases), but we can only survive between 8-14 days without water. Bible INTAKE is essential for a healthy spiritual heart!
- **Exercise** – We cannot have faith in Christ and remain unfruitful. We must exercise our faith by serving Christ and the body of Christ. We use the gifts that have been given to us for the betterment of humanity.

3. Control what you THINK about – 2 Corinthians 10:5

*"casting down arguments and every high thing that exalts itself against the knowledge of God, bringing every thought into captivity to the obedience of Christ."*

As followers of Jesus Christ, we must nix the sins of our thought life. Everything in our minds must be brought into captivity unto the obedience of Christ. It is wrong for us to dwell in the realm of evil imaginations, or evil mischief, or to be plotting in our minds with the intent to do evil.

Don't miss this – God desires that we dwell upon good things, and not evil. We are challenged throughout the Scripture to dwell on that which is good. I challenge all of us, including myself, to pull down that which exalts itself against God. Don't allow your mind to go there any longer.

There are times I find my thoughts going places where they shouldn't be, and I stop and say, "That's not a godly thought." And I seek to pull that thought down and to bring it into captivity. Obedience to Christ is the key!

What are you and I to think about? Paul wrote,

*"Finally, brethren, whatever things are true, whatever things are noble, whatever things are just, whatever things are pure, whatever things are lovely, whatever things are of good report, if there is any virtue and if there is anything praiseworthy—meditate on these things."* (Philippians 4:8)

We can guard the redeemed heart by being careful about what we allow our minds to dwell upon.

### Wrap Up

I believe that there must be some practical take-home truths. How do we take what we have read and actually apply it to our daily lives?

**1. We must have a longing for that state of innocence.**

There is not one of us who would want to live in this world forever. No, we long for something better, and we who have faith in God believe that God will provide us with a better place. There is coming a day when we will once again be fully in a state of innocence. What a day that will be!

*Your First Day In Heaven*

CHORUS
Well it's a great, great mornin'
Your first day in Heaven,
When you stroll down the Golden Avenue.
There are mansions left and right
And you're thrilled at every sight
And the saints are always smiling sayin', "How do you do?"
Oh it's a great, great mornin'
You're first day in Heaven,
When you realize your worryin' day are through.
You'll be glad you were not idol,
Took time to read your Bible,
It's a great mornin' for you.
I had a dream, I must confess, I hated to awake.
He dreamt he was an angel at the great pearly gates.
Saint Peter said, "Well hello there, where have you been?
We've got your mansion ready so come right in."
And then he rang for an angel to act as a guide.
He spread his wings a time or two and learned how to fly.

CHORUS
It's a great mornin',
A great mornin'
What a happy day.[2]

## 2. We must STOP making excuses for our bent on devising wicked plans.

Why is it that people have such a hard time acknowledging that they are broken, that they inherited from their parents, who inherited it from their parents, all the way back to Adam and Eve, a total brokenness of the heart?

Why do we always look for and come up with excuses for our devising wicked imaginations? We looked at 12 excuses from the life of Adam and Eve. Has it occurred to us that our excuses have already been used? Nothing new under the Sun – God has heard it all.

Determine today, right now, at this very moment whose voice you are going to hear. Walk away from this chapter determined to listen to the voice of God – refuse all other voices.

**3. We must allow God to redeem our hearts, and give us New Hearts.**

Have you placed your complete trust in the person of Jesus Christ for Salvation? This is where all true hope is discovered. If you have received Jesus Christ as your Savior, then you have experienced a HEART TRANSPLANT, and you have received the Holy Spirit of God. He has taken up residence inside of you. My question is simple: Does He Show?

You and I have a responsibility before God to guard our hearts; to keep a heart-healthy spiritual life. I believe that the best way to do this is to allow God to be a part of everything we do – I mean everything!

The heart is the center of who we are, and God is to be the center of who we are, and when we understand this, soon we begin to have God's PLANS for our life, and that is true spiritual freedom.

End Notes:

[1]     http://www.herbal-home-remedies.com/blog/272/10-major-effects-of-heart-disease-on-the-body/

[2] More lyrics: http://www.lyricsmode.com/lyrics/i/imperials/#share

# CHAPTER 6
# FEET THAT ARE SWIFT IN RUNNING TO EVIL

I n this chapter, we will turn our attention to the sixth thing that the Lord hates. In Proverbs 6:16-19 we read,

*"These six things the Lord hates, Yes, seven are an abomination to Him: A proud look, A lying tongue, Hands that shed innocent blood, A heart that devises wicked plans, <u>Feet that are swift in running to evil</u>, A false witness who speaks lies,   And one who sows discord among brethren."*

I have had you write in the margin of your Bible keywords that would help us quickly understand this section of Scripture whenever we might come across it in our Bible reading. The words you should have are:

- **Pride**
- **Lying**
- **Murder**
- **Wickedness** (Imaginations)

Now, once again in the margin of your Bible, I want you to write the word: "Evil". Did you do it? I have you do this so that when you are reading through Proverbs you will easily spot this section of Scripture, and have the ability to recall what you have learned. I also want you to be able to teach others. Pass along to someone else what you are learning from Proverbs 6:16-19.

These are the things that the LORD hates, and things we are to hate.

In Proverbs 6:18b, we read,

*"Feet that are swift in running to evil,"*

Those words can literally be translated,

- *Feet that move quickly into sin.*
- *Hurrying to run to evil.*
- *Feet that run rapidly to evil.*
- *Feet that are swift in running to mischief.*

When we contemplate the words *"feet that are swift"* we must understand that we are not looking at people who have simply fallen into sin, but those who actually show an eagerness to do what is wrong. They have an eagerness to seize the opportunity to do evil.

It has been said that "feet follow where the heart has already been." How true it is! Perhaps you have found it true in your life as well. Do you know anyone who seems to always allow their feet to take them into places of evil?

How can we as followers of Jesus Christ avoid allowing our feet to run swiftly to evil?

### I. Know the Problem With our Feet

In Proverbs 1:15-16, we read,

*"My son, walk not thou in the way with them; refrain thy foot from their path: For their feet run to evil, and make haste to shed blood."*

Don't walk with those who are going down the path of evil.

The prophet Isaiah penned the following words,

*"Their feet run to evil, And they make haste to shed innocent blood; Their thoughts are thoughts of iniquity; Wasting and destruction are in their paths."* (Isaiah 59:7)

We really don't get the full meaning of this single verse until we go back and read it in its total context. I want us to take a look at Isaiah 59:1-8, and afterward, I want us to see how closely it appears to connect with the seven things that God hates found in Proverbs 6:16-19.

In this Isaiah 59 passage, we have the execution of premeditated acts of sin. We read about people who allow their feet to run to evil, who make haste to shed innocent blood. Did you know that of the Americans who are now alive, some 2,000,000 will be murdered? They will be killed by people whose feet are swift to run to evil.

As followers of Jesus, we MUST be careful who our friends are. The Bible teaches that *"bad company corrupts good morals"* (2 Corinthians 15:33). If you are friends with someone who only runs into evil, then it is time for you to make different friends.

Andy Stanley says, "Friends determine the direction and the quality of your life."

Peer pressure is powerful – as a follower of Jesus Christ, you and I are to be the more powerful peer! Friends influence one another, but the believer is to be the more powerful influencer! Instead of having feet that are swift in running to evil, we ought to have feet that are swift to run to good.

If you find yourself involved in evil things (things contrary to the holiness of God) then it is time you STOP in your tracks and make some necessary changes. Take the High Road! The Bible calls it the NARROW ROAD (Matthew 7:13-14).

I want us to turn to Romans 3:9-20, and I would like to read these verses as I believe they show us the depth of the problem when it comes to our feet. Focus especially on verse 15, when we get there.

*"Their feet are swift to shed blood;"*

For many young people in Fort Worth, Texas, September 15, 1999, started with prayer around their high school's flagpole. After taking a public stand for their faith, about 400 youth gathered in the sanctuary of Wedgwood Baptist Church for a See-You-at-the-Pole rally that night. Alleluias rang out as a Christian band led the group in singing praises. Suddenly a lone gunman burst in. Larry Ashbrook killed seven people before committing suicide. At first, many thought the gunman was part of a skit. But they soon realized the bullets weren't blanks and the blood wasn't ketchup.

Our feet have a major problem. We must acknowledge the problem with our feet. Our feet often want to take us places where we should never go. What is the answer? This brings us to our second point:

## II. Know the Purpose of our Feet

Feet are used throughout the Bible. It is a very interesting study. Try it sometime. Grab yourself a Bible Concordance, and look up the word *"feet"*. You can literally spend a few hours reading and searching what the Bible has to say about feet.

For example:

- When God spoke to Moses in the wilderness, he was instructed to take off his sandals and to stand before Him barefooted (Exodus 3:5).
- In Ezekiel, people pounded the ground with their feet out of extreme joy (Ezekiel 6:11; 25:6).
- When a king conquered people, the leaders would be brought before him and he would place his feet on their necks (Joshua 10:24, Psalm 110:1). When the culmination of

all things occur, this is what Jesus is going to do for us – our feet will crush Satan (Romans 16:20, 1 Corinthians 15:25).
- Listeners and pupils sat at their master's feet: Mary at Jesus' feet (Luke 10:39); Paul at Gamaliel's feet (Acts 22:3).

With all the information that I studied about feet, I came up with two very practical purposes for our feet. Are you ready to receive these two truths?

1. Feet are to be used to bring forth Good News

In the book of Isaiah, we read,

*"How beautiful upon the mountains Are the feet of him who brings good news, Who proclaims peace, Who brings glad tidings of good things, Who proclaims salvation, Who says to Zion, "Your God reigns!"* (Isaiah 52:7)

The simple truth is that feet carry the messenger, who carries the message!

In the book of Romans, we read,

*"How then shall they call on Him in whom they have not believed? And how shall they believe in Him of whom they have not heard? And how shall they hear without a preacher? And how shall they preach unless they are sent? As it is written: "How beautiful are the feet of those who preach the gospel of peace, Who bring glad tidings of good things!"* (Romans 10:14-15)

I would like to suggest to all of us that we are to have the feet of evangelists. We are the messengers of God on earth today, and each one of us is called by God to carry forth the Good News of Jesus Christ to a lost and dying world.

When the world talks about bad news, let us speak about the Good News! True hope is found only in the person of Jesus Christ.

2. Feet are to be used in mentoring others in Christianity

Every one of us needs at least three types of people in our lives, according to Dr. Howard Hendricks. He has written that we need:

1. **We need a Paul** – Paul will be our teacher and instructor. It is here where we sit at the feet of our teachers. Who's feet are you sitting at? Who is your teacher of the faith? You need one.
2. **We need a Barnabas** – Barnabas will walk with us in the role of an encourager. Every believer also needs to have someone who God will bring into their life to uplift and encourage them. I am so thankful for those that God has brought into my life.
3. **We need a Timothy** – Timothy is who we can mentor, someone to sit at your feet. Who is the person God has in your life right now that you are to be an example to?

I have already mentioned to you that listeners and pupils sat at their master's feet: Disciples sat at the feet of Jesus, as did crowds. We read that Mary sat at Jesus' feet (Luke 10:39), and that Paul sat at Gamaliel's feet (Acts 22:3). All learners need to be at the feet of their teachers!

Get this down: You are a master teacher in some areas. Do you have any students? If you do, great! However, if you don't, why not? Our church is filled with people of all ages that need a godly TEACHER! We need ROLE MODELS!

### Discipleship is the Program of the Bible

Not only do we need to know the purpose of our feet, but just like a doctor who pulls out his writing pad to scribble off a prescription, you and I need to have a prescription for our feet. This brings us to our final point in this message.

### III. Know the Prescription for our Feet

## Mistrusting Own Feet

There is a Chinese story about a man from Cheng who was about to buy a pair of shoes. He measured the length of his feet but forgot to take the measurement with him when he went to the marketplace. "I must go back and get my measurement," he said to the shoe man when he discovered his oversight and forthwith went back home. When he returned to the market, the market had already closed. "Why didn't you try the shoes with your feet?" someone asked him. "I'd rather trust my measurement than my feet," was his reply. —Chinese Humor[1]

That's funny, but there is an excellent truth there. The measurement for the Believer is the Word of God. We must always trust the measurement over our feet. Our feet can carry us to places that the Scripture entirely forbids! Trust the measurement!

I want to provide for us a five-fold prescription for our feet today, based on what the Bible alone teaches. Are you ready to receive it, and apply it to your feet today? Here it is:

1. Restrain your feet – Psalm 119:101

*"I have restrained my feet from every evil way, That I may keep Your word." (Psalm 119:101)*

The KJV uses the word "refrained". Here the NKJV uses the word "restrained". What does this word mean? It means that we refuse, withhold, to keep ourselves from doing, feeling, or indulging in something, especially following a passing impulse.

Allow me to provide you with a HIT HOME illustration. We can all relate to this: Suppose that you have a weight problem, or that you are a person given to impulse eating. To restrain or refrain means that you do not reach for that dessert. You keep yourself from partaking in it.

The world may run to evil, but as followers of Jesus Christ our whole being ought to desire to keep God's Word. The Scripture should have preeminence in our lives!

2. Let the Word guide your feet – Psalm 119:105

There are actually three key verses that I want to pass along to you in regard to allowing the Bible to guide our feet. Too often we make our decisions based upon impulse, feelings, and desires, and we never ever consider the WORD of God.

Is the Bible your guidebook? Do you base where your feet take you on the Scripture?

Listen again to what God's Word teaches us:

- *"Your word is a lamp to my feet And a light to my path."* (Psalm 119:105)

The Bible is pictured as a lamp. What do you use a lamp for? You use it to find your way in the dark. Now, the Bible also teaches that you and I live in a world that is full of darkness. We need a lamp to keep us from stumbling in the dark.

This verse also tells us that the Bible is a light to "my" path. The Psalmist personalized this truth, and so we must do it, also. Do we allow the Scripture to light up the path that we are walking on? Do we ask the question: What does the Bible say about this?

- *"I thought about my ways, And turned my feet to Your testimonies."* (Psalm 119:59)

This is a great verse, and I believe that we have a tremendous contrast before us. Look at the words:

**My ways – Your testimonies**

If you recall from our last study, our hearts can come up with some very wicked plans. Much of our ways are established by our thought life. I would like to suggest that this verse is teaching us to contemplate where our thoughts might be taking us, and to always make the Scripture the final authority! In other words, my thoughts might want to carry my feet in one direction, but my feet will walk only in the direction that God's word points them.

This is extremely difficult, especially if you are not in the Bible regularly. As followers of Jesus Christ, we must allow the Scripture to reign in us.

What will it be for you – your ways or God's word?

In Proverbs 3:21-26 we learn,

*"My son, let them not depart from your eyes— Keep sound wisdom and discretion; So they will be life to your soul and grace to your neck. Then you will walk safely in your way, And your foot will not stumble. When you lie down, you will not be afraid; Yes, you will lie down and your sleep will be sweet. Do not be afraid of sudden terror, Nor of trouble from the wicked when it comes; For the Lord will be our confidence, And will keep your foot from being caught."*

These verses are full of promises for those who will allow the Bible to guide them through the path of life.

- Allow the Bible a place in your life and it will be life to you.
- Allow the Bible a place in your life and you will walk safely in your ways.
- Allow the Bible a place in your life and your foot will not stumble.
- Allow the Bible a place in your life and when you sleep, it will be sweet.
- Allow the Bible a place in your life and you will not fear when trouble comes your way.

- Allow the Bible a place in your life and God will keep your foot from being caught (snares of the wicked).

## 3. Consider where your feet are taking you - Proverbs 4:26-27

*"Ponder the path of your feet, And let all your ways be established. Do not turn to the right or the left; Remove your foot from evil."* (Proverbs 4:26-27)

The word *"ponder"* literally means "to weigh." We have all heard people say, "I am weighing my options." Well, may I suggest that we take the needed time to weigh out the consequences that may follow when you allow your feet to take you to a certain place?

The words *"the path of your feet"* are speaking about the directions we take in life or the teachings we are open to, or it may also mean the rutted path we often get stuck in. Ever feel that you are stuck in a rut? Do you want out of the rutted path?

One of the major problems with Christianity today is that few Christians have the ability to keep their focus. We are challenged in this verse to not turn to the right or to the left. The idea is that we are to look straight (see Luke 9:62). The Bible says,

*"looking unto Jesus, the author and finisher of our faith,"* (Hebrews 12:2)

Over and over, time and time again the authors of the Bible write that our focus must constantly stay on Jesus. He is the THEME of the entire Bible. Keep your eyes straight before you and your feet will carry you to the place where you will be established. Your life and the Bible will match!

What if this has not been your practice? What if you have been turning every which way? Well, the verse says, *"Remove your foot from evil."* You can't get any clearer than that. To "Remove" means to change the direction you have been walking, to change positions, or to change stations.

## 4. Allow Jesus Christ to guide your feet – Luke 2:41-49

Take a moment and open your Bible to Luke 2:41-49. Here before us, we have the account of Mary, Joseph, and Jesus traveling to Jerusalem for the Feast of the Passover. Jesus was twelve years old at the time. When they had finished, Mary and Joseph were headed home. They had been traveling a day's journey when they realized that Jesus wasn't with them. They looked for Him among their relatives and acquaintances but did not find Him, so they returned to Jerusalem seeking Him. After searching for three days they found Him in the temple where He was in discussion with teachers. His parents were amazed at what they found their son doing, but they also got after Him. Mary said to Jesus, *"Son, why have you done this to us? Look, Your father and I have sought you anxiously."* Do you think that Jesus' parents were a little concerned about their son? I think so. Listen to how Jesus responds to them in verse 49,

*"And He said to them, "Why did you seek Me? Did you not know that I must be about My Father's business?"*

May I ask you a question? Are your feet about your Father's business? We need to allow Jesus Christ to guide our feet. He set before us an example to follow.

5. Make straight paths for your feet - Hebrews 12:13

*"and make straight paths for your feet, so that what is lame may not be dislocated, but rather be healed."* (Hebrews 12:13)

Once again I just want us to consider the words, *"make straight paths for your feet"*. Do we recognize the fact that our feet will either cause great harm to those around us or bring about healing? People will either be adversely affected by where we allow our feet to take us, or they will greatly benefit from the example we have set with our feet.

May God help us to be the latter!

**Wrap Up**

We are to hate that which God hates, and He hates *"feet that are swift in running to evil."*

I have provided us with a simple and logical understanding of both the size of the problem we face, as well as the solution. Most of us are aware of the problem – we see it all around us. However, will we apply the solution? Will we follow God's purpose for our feet? And will we pull out the five-fold PRESCRIPTION and follow it?

Our feet will be the telltale sign as to what we do with what we have read!

Where will your feet take you?

End Notes:

[1] Tan, P. L. (1996). Encyclopedia of 7700 Illustrations: Signs of the Times. Garland, TX: Bible Communications, Inc.

# CHAPTER 7
# A FALSE WITNESS THAT SPEAKS LIES

H ave you ever had someone tell a lie about you – told someone something about you that wasn't true? How did that make you feel? People have lost reputations and jobs because of a false witness that speaks lies.

In this chapter we will be looking at the sixth thing that the LORD hates, and that we are to hate. We find it in Proverbs 6:19a, and we read,

"_A false witness who speaks lies_, And one who sows discord among brethren."

Now, in the margin of your Bible, I want you to write the word: Falsehood.

Two times in four verses we are told that God hates lying. No other sin is listed twice. Why do you suppose that this particular sin is listed twice? Is it possible that it is because of the propensity of this sin in all of our lives? I think so!

In verse 17, we have a person who lies through their teeth, and in verse 19, we have an individual who lies through their teeth against another.

What is a false witness? It is when a person perjures themselves by making a statement that is not true. It is a person who makes damaging statements about others that are not true. False witnesses have ruined the lives of innocent people more times than we probably can even conceive with our minds.

### I. The Facts – People Lie About Others

Have you ever been falsely accused? How did it make you feel?

Listen to how a false witness is described in picture form by the author of the book of Proverbs. Proverbs 25:18,

*"A man who bears false witness against his neighbor Is like a club, a sword, and a sharp arrow."*

People who bear false witness against another are pictured as a club, a sword, or a sharp arrow. None of which sound very inviting!

There is a book out on the market called, *The New Doublespeak: Why No One Knows What Anyone's Saying Anymore* by William Lutz. I have read an excerpt from the book, and it mentions the following as an example of the doublespeak we so often hear today. Consider the following examples:

- A tax increase is actually portrayed as "revenue enhancement".
- Being fired is not fired, but you're being "transitioned" or "uninstalled".
- Political lies are called "strategic misrepresentations," "reality augmentation," or "terminological inexactitudes."
- Ordinary sewage sludge becomes "regulated organic nutrients".

- A recession is a "meaningful downturn in aggregate output".
- Kick-back is "after-sales service".
- A trash dump is a "resource development park".
- Stolen goods are "temporarily displaced inventory".

It's this last one that I want to mention that flows in the direction of this chapter. Hear this one:

- **Lying** is "strategic misrepresentation" or "Reality augmentation"[1]

False witnesses and their lies are discovered throughout the Bible. We need to always remember that Satan is the first liar and that he is the father of all lies (John 8:44). Here is a list that I came up with about various individuals in the Bible who were victims of false witnesses who spoke lies against them.

- **Joseph**, by Potiphar's wife - Genesis 39:14–18.
- **Naboth** – 1 Kings 21:8-13
- **David** – Psalm 27:12
- **Nehemiah** – Nehemiah 6
- **Daniel** – Daniel 6:24
- **Jeremiah**, by the Jews – Jeremiah 18:18
- **Jesus** – Matthew 26:59-61, Mark 14:55-59[2]

*"Now the chief priests, and elders, and all the council, sought false witness against Jesus, to put him to death; [60] But found none: yea, though many false witnesses came, yet found they none. At the last came two false witnesses, [61] And said, This fellow said, I am able to destroy the temple of God, and to build it in three days."*

*"Jesus answered and said unto them, Destroy this temple, and in three days I will raise it up. Then said the Jews, Forty and six years was this*

*temple in building, and wilt thou rear it up in three days? [21] But he spoke of the temple of his body."* (John 2:19-21)

- **Disciples** – Matthew 28:12-15
- **Stephen** - Acts 6:11-14
- **Paul** – Acts 17:5-7, 24:5-9, 25:7; Romans 3:8

Here is a TRUTH that will blow your mind: As followers of Jesus Christ we are NOT to be false witnesses, but we will be victims of false witnesses. If the saints of old did not escape, do we really believe we can?

Jesus taught his disciples the following,

*"Blessed are you when they revile and persecute you, <u>and say all kinds of evil against you falsely for My sake.</u> Rejoice and be exceedingly glad, for great is your reward in heaven, for so they persecuted the prophets who were before you."* (Matthew 5:11-12)

Mark Twain is quoted as saying, "One of the striking differences between a cat and a lie is a cat only has nine lives." False statements continue to live and continue to spread and continue to do great damage.

Martin Luther, the great reformer, said, "A lie is like a snowball. The longer it's rolled on the ground, the bigger it becomes."

The facts are quite obvious – people spread lies about one another!

## II. The Truth – God's Word Sets People Straight

Can you answer the following question for me: Are God's people (believers) to be different from the rest of humanity? Yes! None of us should even have to be hesitant to answer that question. The fact that we have been born again should have a dramatic effect in all areas of our lives! One such area is that we do NOT bear false witness against our neighbors, or anyone else.

What does the Bible have to teach us about false witnesses? We learn the following:

A. It goes against God's Commandment - Exodus 20:16

*"Thou shalt not bear false witness against thy neighbor."*

St. Augustine had a sign on his desk that declared: *"Whosoever enters this office to bring an accusation against his brother will be ushered out of this room."* Augustine took this Commandment seriously. He declared, *"The tongue inflicts greater wounds than the sword."*

B. It is an evil that was to be done away with – Deuteronomy 19:16-21

*"If a false witness rises against any man to testify against him of wrong-doing, then both men in the controversy shall stand before the Lord, before the priests and the judges who serve in those days. And the judges shall make careful inquiry, and indeed, if the witness is a false witness, who has testified falsely against his brother, then you shall do to him as he thought to have done to his brother; <u>so you shall put away the evil from among you.</u> And those who remain shall hear and fear, and hereafter they shall not again commit such evil among you. Your eye shall not pity: life shall be for life, eye for eye, tooth for tooth, hand for hand, foot for foot."*

C. It is seen as putting your hand with the wicked - Exodus 23:1-3

*"You shall not circulate a false report. <u>Do not put your hand with the wicked to be an unrighteous witness.</u> You shall not follow a crowd to do evil; nor shall you testify in a dispute so as to turn aside after many to pervert justice. You shall not show partiality to a poor man in his dispute.*

D. It will be severely judged by God - Psalm 101:5-7

*"Whoever secretly slanders his neighbor, <u>Him I will destroy;</u> The one who has a haughty look and a proud heart, Him I will not endure. My eyes shall be on the faithful of the land, That they may dwell with me; He who walks in a perfect way, He shall serve me. He who works deceit shall not*

*dwell within my house; He who tells lies shall not continue in my presence."*

E. It will not go unpunished - Proverbs 19:5 (see also verse 9)

*"A false witness will not go unpunished, And he who speaks lies will not escape."*

F. It was taught as a no-no by Jesus Christ - Matthew 19:18[3]

*"He said to Him, "Which ones?" Jesus said, "'You shall not murder,' 'You shall not commit adultery,' 'You shall not steal,' '<u>You shall not bear false witness,</u>'"*

The masses may say, "it's no big deal," but the Bible says that God hates it, and as followers of Jesus Christ we are to HATE what God HATES, whether you're the President, the Pastor, or the parishioner. God hates lying, no matter how we dress it up.

### III. The Decision – We Must Choose to Be Different

The late Robert G. Lee wrote,

One mischievous boy can break up a school. One false alarm can cause panic. One match can start a conflagration. One false step can cost a life or ruin a character. One broken wheel can ditch a train. One quarrelsome worker can create a strike of ten thousand men.

One undiplomatic word can provoke a war involving thousands of lives and the destruction of millions of dollars in property. One hasty act of legislation can entail untold hardships. One wayward daughter can break a mother's heart. One lie can destroy a person's character. One false witness can send an innocent man to jail. One vote can decide an election.

One kind word at the right time may save a person from suicide. One sermon may fire a man's soul and set the course for his future life. One drink may start a person on the road to alcoholism. One wrong example may lead dozens down the wrong path. One decision for Christ will determine future destiny. [4]

Ecclesiastes 9:18 states,

*"One sinner destroyeth much good"*

In the classroom setting of one Peanuts comic strip, on the first day of the new school year, the students were told to write an essay about returning to class. In her essay, Lucy wrote, "Vacations are nice, but it's good to get back to school. There is nothing more satisfying or challenging than education, and I look forward to a year of expanding knowledge." Needless to say, the teacher was pleased with Lucy and complimented her fine essay. In the final frame, Lucy leans over and whispers to Charlie Brown, "After a while, you learn what sells."

We can be the *"one sinner that destroys much good"*, and we can be like Lucy, who knows *"what sells"*, or we can choose to be different. We can choose to be Christian. I would hope that each one of us would make the decision to speak the truth.

In Proverbs 12:17 we have a contrast between two choices,

*"He who speaks truth declares righteousness, But a false witness, deceit."*

What will it be for us today? Which side of this verse will we decide to live our lives by? Let's draw the line in the sand today. On which side of the line will you take your stand? There are only two options: Truth vs. Deceit.

### DECEIT
*"But a false witness, deceit."*

### TRUTH
*"He who speaks truth declares righteousness,"*

Do we understand that **we will STAND somewhere**? So, where will we stand? To decide right now NOT to decide is still a decision! As followers of Jesus Christ, we cannot waffle on a topic of this importance. As a Pastor, I am calling each one of us to "SPEAK

TRUTH", and "declare righteousness". Stand for TRUTH, and NEVER fall on the side of those who use deceit against another person.

## Wrap Up

God hates a false witness that speaks lies, and so should the follower of Jesus Christ.

As followers of Jesus Christ, we are not to lie about others. We are to be different from the world – the world has no godly values, but the Christian does. This is what makes Christianity radical!

1. The Facts are obvious – People lie about others.

Many great people throughout the ages have been lied about – from Joseph to Jesus, and Naboth to Paul.

Puritan preacher Thomas Watson taught: *"As it is a sin against this Commandment to raise a false report of another, so it is to receive a false report before you have examined it…he that raises a slander, carries the devil in his tongue; and he that receives it, carries the devil in his ear."*

2. The Truth is solid – God's Word sets people straight.

Lies simply go against everything that is godly!

Christians are to be TRUTH tellers.

3. The Decision is now – We must choose to be different.

The followers of Jesus Christ must make a choice to be different. Let us remember, *"He who speaks truth declares righteousness."*

What will it be for you? Lies or TRUTH?

End Notes:

[1] The New Doublespeak by William Lutz

[2] Of Jesus, by the Jews falsely charging that he was a drunkard, Matt. 11:19; that he blasphemed, Mark 14:64; John 5:18; that he had a devil, John 8:48, 52; 10:20; that he was seditious, Luke 22:65; 23:5; that he was a king, Luke 23:2; John 18:37, with John 19:1–5[2]

[3] Repeated in Luke 10:17-22, Luke 18:18-23

[4] Tan, P. L. (1996). Encyclopedia of 7700 Illustrations: Signs of the Times. Garland, TX: Bible Communications, Inc.

# CHAPTER 8
# HE WHO SOWS DISCORD AMONG HIS BRETHREN

We now come to the last item on God's hate list. It is found here in Proverbs 6:19b. And not only does God hate it, but it is an abomination to Him. We read,

*"And one who sows discord among brethren."*

Look at the word *"sows"*. To sow means to plant the seeds of something. What kind of seeds are you planting in the church? Every one of us is sowing some kind of seeds today - what seeds are we planting within the body of Christ? Seeds of edification, or seeds of destruction?

Now, take a moment and write in the margin of your Bible next to verse 19, the word, "discord".

Discord defined:

- lack of agreement or harmony (as between persons, things, or ideas)
- active quarreling or conflict resulting from discord among persons or factions: strife[1]

Repeat after me: Discord hurts everyone! Do we believe that? Really, do we understand that discord hurts all of the body of Christ?

In a 2000 Faith Communities Today survey of 14,301 churches, 75% of churches reported having some level of conflict in the five years prior, with 25% reporting what they considered to be serious conflict. A follow-up study found that over two-thirds of churches experiencing conflict reported a loss of members as a result, and about 25% suffered the loss of a leader.

The point is clear: Discord affects the body of Christ.

There are three points that I want to drive home in this chapter: First, the warning against discord; second, the various reasons for discord; and thirdly, the solution for overcoming discord.

Let's consider these points now.

**I. The Warning Against Discord.**

Here in Proverbs 6:19b, we have the words,

*"And one who sows discord among brethren."*

I believe that these words are here to warn us who are alive today about those things that God sees as an abomination. Why does God hate "discord"? Because it destroys what He is seeking to establish and build!

This verse warns us against discord.

Below you will discover several examples of discord that I came across in preparation for this chapter. I have provided you the following examples with the intent that it would show us how discord develops, who it hurts, and the end results.

The bottom line I want us to remember is that discord hurts everyone!

## Example # 1 – Red and Green Church Roof

There is a church in Louisiana whose roof is green on one side and red on the other. This was done because some members of the church adamantly wanted green and other members adamantly wanted red. The disagreement was so intense that the church was going to split because of it. Fortunately, a compromise was reached and the church did not split. Unfortunately, the red and green roof is a monument to the surrounding community of the disunity within the body of Christ.

## Example # 2 – Proper Preaching

A pastor went to the home of a congregation member to talk to them about being on the church board. They were regular attendees and faithful givers and their teenage kids were highly involved in the various church programs. Once the conversation began, he immediately came under fire for not preaching the way this couple felt he should theologically. He sat back in the chair with a shocked look on his face, and finally, discreetly, ended the meeting without asking them to join the board. He was devastated.

## Example # 3 – Simultaneous Preaching

There was a news story that came out of Wales that told of a feud in a church looking for a new pastor. It read: "Yesterday the two opposition groups both sent ministers to the pulpit. Both spoke simultaneously, each trying to shout above the other. Both called for hymns, and the congregation sang two—each trying to drown out the other. Then the groups started shouting at each other. Bibles were raised in anger. The Sunday morning service turned into bedlam. Through it all, the two preachers continued trying to outshout each other with their sermons. Eventually, a deacon called a policeman. Two came in and began shouting for the congregation to be quiet. They advised the forty persons in the church to return home. The rivals filed out, still arguing. Last night one of the groups called a let's-be-friends meeting. It broke up in an argument." The story could have been headlined, "Two Factions in One Fellowship." This story may be amusing, but it is also tragic.

## Example # 4 – Choosing a Cross

Many years ago when we were making a choice as to what type of a cross we wanted hanging above the baptistry here at SLBC, the congregation was given two choices: 1. A smooth wood cross. 2. A rough wooden cross. Once the church voted, and the decision was made one lady got up and walked out extremely upset over the decision. Everyone left behind knew she was upset. It could have caused division within the church. However, later that Sunday afternoon, I received a phone call from her, and she made an apology for her outburst of sinful behavior. The choice of the people was carried out.

Do we see the personal damage that discord can bring into a church? Discord not only affects the church, but causes great harm to the testimony of Christ within a community. Somehow we need to remind ourselves that Christianity is not about us!

## II. The Various Causes of Discord.

Are you aware that not everyone who sets foot in the church necessarily has the best interests of the church body in mind? I once had a man boast to me that he was responsible for having a pastor at another church removed from office (I was wondering what he was telling me). Do you know why he was involved in removing the pastor? One day the pastor spotted his little girl doing something wrong, and he corrected her. For that reason, this man began his agenda to have the pastor removed. He was successful, and today that man is no longer in ministry.

There is a church that I know of in Spokane where this recently played out. They called a man with a doctorate degree to be their pastor. Some didn't like the way he preached, or the length of time he preached, and so one person took it upon themselves to begin a survey among the membership asking questions that were open ended, and which could be interpreted many different ways, but always in a way that made the pastor out as the bad guy. Needless to say, after a lengthy period of time the pastor was sent packing. Discord can ruin a church and a pastorate.

With over forty-plus years of ministry behind me I have discovered that most issues that arise within the church are over personalities, or over personal desires; very few are over legitimate heretical issues When someone is not getting their way, they go on the offense and begin to sow discord within the body of Christ. If you ever find yourself trying to get people within the church to side with you on a certain decision, and you begin to make remarks that are defamatory against another brother/sister in Christ then you are sowing discord among brethren; and as we are learning, God hates it!

There are several reasons as to why discord can spread within the church. Allow me to share with you some of the top causes:

1. Differing backgrounds.

The church is made up of people from all over the spectrum of life. Our social, ethnic, cultural, and economic backgrounds are all different. The church is very diverse, and its diversity can either be a major blessing or a major problem. We might have grown up in a certain setting and, well, we expect that setting to be the way things are where we attend church.

2. Differing preferences.

There have literally been thousands of church problems based on personal preferences. Many times personal preferences separate people into various divisions or camps. These camps seek to evangelize others to their cause, and thus soon one camp has a majority, and if others are unwilling to join them, well, the inevitable happens – the church **SPLITS**!

Such preferences surround things like:

- Clothing styles
- Television and movies
- Card playing
- Translations used in the church
- Offering bag (closed), or offering tray (open)
- Music – contemporary or hymns
- Preaching – expository or topical

I remember reading some time back about a man who was shipped wrecked on a deserted island. After many years a ship spotted his S.O.S. signal fire and came to his rescue. Before the man left the island, he asked to show the captain around. The captain was impressed with the various buildings that he had pieced together. One question that the captain asked the man was why he had built two churches. The man replied, "Well, one Sunday I had a disagreement and decided that I wasn't able to attend church there anymore, and so I built this second church building."

3. Differing convictions.

I believe with all of my heart that we need convictions, but our convictions must be based on Scripture, and not on personal conviction. I cannot live another person's Christian life, and neither can you. I may have a list of convictions about certain types of situations, but I must always remember that they are "personal convictions." There is a huge difference between personal convictions and doctrinal truth.

Comedian Emo Philips used to tell the following story:

In conversation with a person I had recently met, I asked, "Are you Protestant or Catholic?"

My new acquaintance replied, "Protestant."

I said, "Me too! What franchise?"

He answered, "Baptist."

"Me too!" I said. "Northern Baptist or Southern Baptist?"

"Northern Baptist," he replied.

"Me too!" I shouted.

We continued to go back and forth. Finally, I asked, "Northern conservative fundamentalist Baptist, Great Lakes Region, Council of 1879 or Northern conservative fundamentalist Baptist, Great Lakes Region, Council of 1912?"

He replied, "Northern conservative fundamentalist Baptist, Great Lakes Region, Council of 1912."

I said, "Die, heretic!"

4. Differing personalities.

Most churches have problems with personalities. Someone joins the church who just rubs you the wrong way. There is something about the person that you just don't like. Instead of understanding that God created us all unique, we begin to point out that person's flaws, or inabilities, or we make up some wild story about how they are taking control of everything.

Several years ago a man wrote me a letter and said that my style of leadership when he was growing up was called Communism, and today it is called dictatorship. Wow! Do you know how deeply that hurt?

It takes all kinds of people to make up a church. We are all so different. Some people are:

- Bold – others are timid
- Loquacious – others are quiet

- Organized – others are easygoing
- Rigid – others are pliable
- Teachers – others are evangelists
- Logical – others are intuitive

Do you know what I have to say? It's okay to be you.

5. Differing maturity.

I hope that everyone reading this would realize that not every follower of Jesus Christ is at the same level of spiritual maturity. It has been said, "All believers are saints in position but not all believers are saintly." Do we allow room for growth, or do we believe that once a person is saved they should instantly have a level of maturity that took other saints 30 years to acquire?

Remember, John was revealed as one of the "sons of thunder" (Mark 3:17, Luke 9:54) before he became known as the "apostle of love".

We must allow room for personal spiritual growth in the lives of those with whom we worship. Remember, it takes years for a tree to produce fruit.

6. Differing self-view.

There are times when problems arise in the church over someone thinking more highly of themselves than they really should (Romans 12:3). I don't want to break anyone's bubble today, but none of us are irreplaceable. We are going to die someday, and someone will come in and pick up where we left off.

We must also be careful that low self-esteem is not the root cause of some church problems. Jealousy that others have gifts that we don't possess has led to many church problems. May I remind you that God is the one who gives us our gifts and talents? God can shoulder your anger, but don't take it out on other believers.

Stirring the brethren up is something that God hates! We ought to hate it too!

Allow me to tell you that it is NEVER RIGHT to destroy a church. If your conduct leads to a church division, or a church split then you are guilty of sowing discord. It would be better for you to walk away quietly than to destroy God's church. And please don't tell me that you are the sacred guardian of God's church. I believe that that is the job of the Holy Spirit – not you!

## III. The Solution to Overcoming Discord.

Jesus told us that the opposite of sowing discord is peacemaking! As a matter of fact, in the beatitudes, we read,

*"Blessed are the peacemakers, For they shall be called sons of God."* (Matthew 5:9)

I believe that the duty and responsibility of every saint is to be a peacemaker rather than an agitator.

The followers of Jesus Christ are to be peacemakers! Are you aware that nowhere in the Bible does God say that he hates "peacemakers"? No, the Bible says that God hates those who sow discord.

Jim Sowers (one of our early deacons) used to tell the story about a guy who would speak up at every church meeting when something new was presented. He would shout out, "I'm a-gin it." There was nothing new presented that he wasn't against!

News Flash: We don't always have to be against something!

I want to share with you what some key biblical characters wrote about the solution to overcoming discord within the body of Christ.

A. James warns us against warring for our own desires – James 4:1-3

James the half-brother of Jesus wrote,

*"Where do wars and fights come from among you? Do they not come from your desires for pleasure that war in your members? You lust and do not have. You murder and covet and cannot obtain. You fight and war. Yet you do not have because you do not ask. You ask and do not receive, because you ask amiss, that you may spend it on your pleasures."*

Author Ken Sande, in *The Peace Maker*, writes, "Conflict starts with some kind of desire (I desire)... unmet desires have the potential of working themselves deeper and deeper into our hearts (I demand)...the more we want something the more we think we need and deserve it. And the more we think we are entitled to something, the more convinced we are that we cannot be happy and secure without it. It moves from a desire to demand, and soon becomes an idol. We cross the line, however, when we begin to sinfully judge others, which is characterized by a feeling of superiority, indignation, condemnation, bitterness, or resentment. Sinful judging often involves speculating on others' motives. Most of all, it reveals the absence of genuine love and concern toward them. When these attitudes are present, our judging has crossed the line and we are playing God."

Here is the progression from the author James -

**1. Desire** (not always bad), 2. **Demand** (always bad), 3. **Idol** (always condemned) , 4. **Judging others** (discord starts).

The first solution to discord within the church is to keep a check and balance on our own personal desires. Bear in mind that not all desires are bad; however, out-of-balance and unchecked desires can and will become destructive within the church.

B. Paul tells us to separate from those who sow discord – Romans 16:17-18

*"Now I urge you, brethren, note those who cause divisions and offenses, contrary to the doctrine which you learned, and avoid them. For those who are such do not serve our Lord Jesus Christ, but their own belly, and by smooth words and flattering speech deceive the hearts of the simple."*

As I've written earlier, not everyone who comes to church has the best interests of the church in mind. Many are totally self-centered and only focused on personal gain. These individuals will bring division and offenses into the church.

Paul tells us that we are to *"note"* those who cause divisions. We get our word *"scope"* from it. It means *"to look at, observe, contemplate; to fix one's eyes and attention upon someone or something."* The entire body of Christ needs to keep its eyes open for those who may enter the church with the intent to bring divisions. The idea is that we are to be protective of the church.

Paul also tells us that we are to *"avoid them"* – I would like to go on record to say that if anyone attending church has anything other than Christ's agenda for the body, PLEASE find another church home. Better yet – GET RIGHT with God! To "avoid" means that we do not listen to their divisive talk and communication, nor do we embrace them.

These individuals are NOT serving our Lord Jesus Christ, but again, their own appetite – their own desire. AVOID them!

And may I also challenge us to be careful NOT to be caught up with those who may be using flattering words? Everyone likes to feel special, however, feeling special; by those whose agenda it is to bring about division within the church has devastating results.

I cannot tell you the number of times I have seen the simple (naïve) swayed by those who were fast talkers and who used smooth words. Do you know what is the number one thing these people will say? "You and I can make this a better place. We deserve more than what we are getting. Let's take things into our hands and bring about the needed changes."

C. Jesus prayed for unity among God's people – John 17:20-21

*"I do not pray for these alone, but also for those who will believe in Me through their word; that they all may be one, as You, Father, are in Me,*

*and I in You; <u>that they also may be one in Us, that the world may believe</u>*
<u>*that You sent Me.*</u>"

Jesus prayed for the unity of all of us who are in the church today. We live in a broken world with fallen people, and saints who are not always living righteously. Unity is a virtue that we as a church ought to seek with all of our hearts. Each one of us ought to behave in the church in such a way that we are answers to Jesus' prayer.

There is such power in oneness! So much more can be accomplished in oneness! According to Jesus, there is oneness in the Godhead, and there ought to be oneness in the church.

Please get this down – Oneness in the church is a testimony to the world that God sent Jesus Christ into the world. Because we as a church maintain oneness, the world says, "These are followers of Jesus Christ."

D. Solomon provided some excellent advice – Proverbs 26:20

There is one last solution that I want to share with you that is taken from the writings of Solomon, known as the wisest man who ever lived. He wrote,

*"Where no wood is, there the fire goeth out: so where there is no talebearer, the strife ceaseth."*

If you have even been camping and have built a fire, you know that one of the quickest ways to cause the fire to die out is to separate the pieces of burning wood. If you separate the fuel, the fire will die. If you stop adding fuel to the fire, the fire will die out as well. The point being made here is really simple – Remove the source of fuel and the fire will cease. Look again at the last part of this verse,

*"so where there is no talebearer, the strife ceaseth."*

Another translation reads,

*"without gossip a quarrel dies down."*

Here is a question each one of us must answer: Am I protecting the unity of the church in the bonds of peace, or am I adding fuel to the fire? I would hope that your answer is that you are protecting the unity of the body.

One author shared four steps that all of us must take when the church is going through turbulent times. He said,

- Make sure your primary goal is to glorify God with your thoughts, words, and actions.
- Always keep your emotions under complete control.
- Bathe yourself and the problem in prayer.
- Never take sides.

He continued by saying, "If most church members would operate under these guidelines, we would have fewer church splits."

## Wrap Up

So, there we have it – The seven things that God hates. God hates these sins because they are the complete opposite of Him – God is not proud – He is humble. God does not lie – he speaks the truth. God does not shed innocent blood – He judges righteously. God does not have a heart that devises wicked plans – He plans with our best interest in mind. God does not have feet that are swift to run into evil – He has feet that are holy. God does not bear false witness – He speaks the truth. God does not sow discord – He establishes unity. Why? Because it is God's nature – it is His character!

These sins will show us our true character as well. Who will we choose to be like? Will we choose to be like Christ, or will we choose to be like the devil? How we live will determine our character. Either we will allow the Holy Spirit to develop godly character within us, or we will allow the devil to use our old sinful nature for his pleasure.

Take a look at the following comparisons below, and ask yourself the question: Where do you want to live?

### The Godhead - Father, Son, Holy Spirit

- Humble – Psalm 113:5-6
- Truthful – Deuteronomy 32:4
- Life-giver – I Timothy 6:13
- No sin – I John 1:5
- Holiness – Isaiah 6
- Righteousness – Psalm 129:4
- Unity – Deuteronomy 6:4-5

### The Devil

- Proud – Isaiah 14, Ezekiel 28
- Liar – John 8:44
- Murderer – John 8:44, Genesis 3
- Full of sin – I John 3:8
- Evilness – Matthew 13:19
- Deceit – Revelation 12:9
- Discord –Proverbs 6:19

Oh, how we need to realize that these seven sins all lie on the WRONG side of where God wants us to be living. They are all unlike Christ and they go against everything that God and Christianity stand for.

Paul made a statement that I would like to close this book with. In Romans 12:9b he wrote,

*"Abhor what is evil. Cling to what is good."*

One final story…

### Discord Over Sunday School

## Leadership Choice

In 1981, Roger Faulkner had been a member of a church in a Chicago suburb for nearly two years. He had served as a Sunday School teacher for more than a year when the position of superintendent became available. Roger was excited about Sunday School and felt that he would be an ideal successor to the position. He went to the pastor and shared his vision and desire to serve, but, to his disappointment, the pastor and church board later chose someone else to serve in that post.

Roger was very offended that he wasn't considered for the job, but didn't say anything to the pastor about it. As the weeks wore on, Roger became increasingly negative and critical toward the church and the people. He began to find fault with the new superintendent and the Sunday School program. He began attending services less and less.

Jeff Billings, another Sunday School teacher, began to notice something wrong with Roger. After church one Sunday, Jeff invited Roger out to lunch.

"Is everything Ok?" Jeff asked. "I've noticed that you've been absent a lot lately and I get the feeling that something is wrong."

"Yeah, you might say that," Roger said sarcastically. "I'm fed up with that stupid church and its immature leadership! The Sunday School program stinks and the pastor couldn't preach his way out of a paper bag! Most of the people here are unspiritual and unloving. I'm just not getting fed here anymore, and I'm thinking about leaving!"

Jeff was shocked. "I can't believe what I'm hearing! Just a few weeks ago you were so excited about the church. You used to brag to everyone that this was the greatest church in town. Just two months ago you told me that this was the most loving congregation you'd ever seen. What's happened to change you?"

"It's not me. It's the church that's changed," fumed Roger. "Besides the incompetence of the Sunday School program, let me tell you a few other things I'm upset about..."

For an hour, Jeff was amazed to hear Roger's complaints. For many weeks afterward, he met with Roger several more times, hoping to encourage him, but to no avail. Instead, he began to empathize with Roger's criticisms. It wasn't long until Jeff too began developing negative attitudes and eventually even resigned from Sunday School.

Bill Stedlund, a friend of Jeff's, took notice that both he and Roger were not as active in the church as they used to be. He observed that when they were in attendance, they usually sat together and would often whisper to each other during the services. He realized that something was wrong.

One evening, Bill saw the two at a local restaurant talking with others from the church. He decided to join them. "How's it going, guys?" Bill said. "Wasn't Sunday's service great! Fifteen souls came to the Lord. And what a sermon! Praise the Lord!"

Everyone at the table just looked at each other. "Sorry, we didn't notice," said Jeff smugly. "I guess we were too preoccupied with the serious problems in the church."

"Problems? What problems?" Bill chirped. "Are you guys goofy or what? The church is going terrific. Lives are being changed every Sunday, the church is growing, and the congregation is ecstatic. What's your problem?"

"Apparently you're blinded to the reality of what's really going on," said Roger. "The church is ruled by politics and unspiritual morons who don't care whose feelings they hurt. Besides, the people of this church have more faults than an earthquake zone! And furthermore..."

Bill interrupted, "Whoa, wait just a second! I've been wondering what's wrong with you guys, and now I guess I know. You are the ones who are blinded! You have developed a critical, fault-finding spirit and the Devil has blinded you from being able to see the beauty of what the Lord is doing."

"Roger, I heard you got your feelings hurt when the pastor chose someone else over you for Sunday School Superintendent. But instead of talking with him about it and forgiving him, you developed a bitter, unforgiving spirit! Now the Devil has deceived you into looking for fault in everything. And to make matters worse, you've taken your discontent and spread it to other brethren. This is a serious violation of God's Word. You ought to know that the Bible says God hates those who spread discord among the brethren. The word 'hate' is pretty harsh language coming from God, and the Bible warns of calamity that will come upon those who spread discord (Proverbs 6:14-15). This means you!"

"Spreading discontent is disobedience to God and will not help solve problems, Roger. Gossip and bad-mouthing only makes a situation worse. Just a few weeks ago, Jeff thought everything was going great until you 'illuminated' him. And How many others have you corrupted with your bad attitude?"

Bill continued, "How did Jesus teach that we should resolve our differences with our brethren? You are to go to the persons who have offended you and talk to them privately and resolve your dispute (Matthew 18:15). Did you keep the matter private and go to the pastor? Did you go to others who offended you? No, you didn't. You selfishly chose to spread your complaints and opinions to others to gather their attention and sympathy to your own hurt feelings."

"Roger and Jeff, where in the Bible does Jesus tell His followers to judge, criticize, or condemn our brethren? You can't tell me, because it doesn't say it! However, Jesus did tell you to love and forgive your brethren, to submit, to prefer, to encourage, to dwell together in love and peace, not to bad-mouth one another, and on and on! (John 13:34, Ephesians 4:29-32, 5:21, Romans 12:10, Hebrews 10:25, Ephesians 4:1-3, Titus 3:2)."

Roger and Jeff were offended by Bill's lecture and thereafter avoided his fellowship. But months later Roger became convicted about his sinful attitude and realized that this was why the Lord had not been answering his prayers. *"If I regard iniquity in my heart, The Lord will not hear"* (Psalm 66:18). He repented of his sin and asked the Lord to forgive him. A few days later he went to the pastor and the other Christians whom he had bad-mouthed and asked for forgiveness. Roger recovered from his troubles and continues to serve the Lord to this day.

Sadly, the person whom Roger had influenced most, Jeff, became more critical and bitter. The discord had taken root and had severely damaged Jeff's faith. Unfortunately, discord is like a bad apple that will spoil the whole barrel — an infection that the Devil uses to spread his evil disease.

Jeff continued to spread the seeds of discord. Dozens left the church and the discontent spread, severely damaging the ministry. Souls ceased coming to the altar for salvation, and the loss of tithers caused the church to struggle for several years. Jeff also had many heartaches and no longer serves God.

Christians must never forget that their words can promote life or death, unity or division, love or hate. Although Roger was forgiven for his evil words sown, his mouth was an instrument of murder to his friend, Jeff, and others. Satan used his mouth to nearly destroy a whole church. How many souls have been murdered with the mouths of discontent believers? "The hypocrite with his mouth destroys his neighbor..." (Proverbs 11:9). The Bible clearly warns us to mark those who cause division and strife and to avoid them. They are used by the Devil to cause trouble to the church and to the work of the Gospel (Romans 16:17).[2]

End Notes:

[1] Merriam-Webster, I. (2003). Merriam-Webster's collegiate dictionary. (Eleventh ed.). Springfield, Mass.: Merriam-Webster, Inc.

[2] Dr. *Dale A. Robbin, Sowing and Reaping the Seeds of Discord,* http://www.victorious.org/discord.htm

# ABOUT THE AUTHOR

Kim J. Alexander has been married to Debbie for 42 years, father of five fantastic children, grandfather to two wonderful grandsons (Derrek & Theophilus), and five beautiful granddaughters (Liesel, Blakely, Amberlynn, Reghan, and Victory), pastor of a great Church (Spirit Lake Baptist) for 28 years, and a Bible teacher (his ultimate passion). Kim holds a Master of Theological Studies from Louisiana Baptist Theological Seminary. Kim loves to explore new places, enjoys writing, and really likes warm weather. He is a two-time Spartan trifecta finisher along with his wife.

*For more information:*
www.slbc2u.org
grace2u4@gmail.com

# ALSO BY KIM ALEXANDER

All books available at Amazon.com

### The Alexander Old Testament Commentaries:

**Ecclesiastes:** Finding Meaning to Life Under the Sun

**Jonah:** God's Reluctant Prophet

### The Alexander New Testament Commentaries:

**Galatians:** Liberty in Jesus Christ Alone

**Colossians:** Complete in Him

**Hebrews 1-10:** The Superiority of Jesus Christ

**Hebrews 11-13:** The Superiority of Jesus Christ

**First John:** Fellowship with God and With Other Believers

**Revelation:** The Unveiling

### Marriage

**two becoming ONE:** Building a Strong Foundation for Marriage

### Christian Life

**Breaking Bad:** Overcoming the Old Nature

**Believer's Boot Camp:** 13 Chapters of Strength Training for a Life Time of Following Jesus

Made in the USA
Monee, IL
08 May 2023

33293113R00076